From Sinners to Saints

FROM
SINNERS
TO SAINTS

ROBERT WERNER

WITH MAUREEN RANK

While this book is intended for the reader's personal enjoyment and profit, it is also intended for group study. A Leader's Guide with Victor Multiuse Transparency Masters is available from your local bookstore or from the publisher.

VICTOR BOOKS ®

A DIVISION OF SCRIPTURE PRESS PUBLICATIONS INC.
USA CANADA ENGLAND

Unless otherwise noted, Scripture quotations are from *New American Standard Bible,* © the Lockman Foundation 1960, 1962, 1963, 1968, 1971, 1972, 1973, 1975, 1977. Scripture quotations marked KJV are taken from *Authorized (King James) Version.*

Recommended Dewey Decimal Classification: 234.3
Suggested Subject Heading: CONVERSION—CHRISTIANITY

Library of Congress Catalog Card Number: 89-060140
ISBN: 0-89693-723-2

CONTENTS

FOREWORD

Congratulations! You have just opened a book which could change your life for the better!

My friend Dr. Bob Werner has done a masterful job of presenting the Gospel message through a series of first-century events recorded in the Scriptures. He brings to this volume thirty years of experience as pastor, evangelist, counselor, and teacher.

Perhaps you're not religious. Maybe you have a weak religious affiliation, or maybe you are fully committed to serve the risen Lord. Whatever your progress in this journey we call life, there is something in this book to help you along the way.

In each chapter you will find easy-to-read, relevant illustrations. Single adults will draw inspiration from these pages, and the spouse whose mate avoids church attendance like the plague will also find encouragement here. The Bible teacher will discover a wealth of material that will enliven any presentation of the Scriptures.

Bob Werner has demonstrated how God uses the one Gospel to reach all types of people in distinctive ways.

Read and reread this work. It will enrich your knowledge and enhance your usefulness. I hope and pray this book will be used extensively in churches and Bible study groups.

I plan to present this book to friends as a gift. Its value will continue long after chocolates have been eaten and flowers have faded.

Dr. John Haggai
Atlanta, Georgia

INTRODUCTION

There seems to be a great deal of confusion today about the real meaning of conversion. This book is an attempt to elimimate that confusion. I have not taken an academic or a theological approach, but rather I have allowed the personalities of the New Testament to come alive and speak for themselves. The cast of characters includes a soldier, a prostitute, a fisherman, a tax official, and a successful businesswoman. It sounds just like a cross section of people in today's society. They each had their own needs and personality, so they came to Christ in unique ways. Their struggles and joys will remind you of people that you know. In fact, you will no doubt be able to relate your own conversion experience to the conversion of one of these New Testament characters. It is my hope that this book will not only strengthen and help clarify your concept of conversion but also help you to reach those who have yet to discover this marvelous experience.

Bob Werner

CHAPTER ONE
Zaccheus—The Outsider

Perhaps you've heard the biblical account of Zaccheus, the little man who climbed a sycamore tree to see Jesus. You may have also heard about the nervous ministerial student who chose Zaccheus' story as the text for his final exam in Preaching 101. In order to complete the course, each of the students had to prepare a three-point sermon applying a Bible lesson to contemporary life. Since he was barely passing already, the young man knew he'd have to give that sermon, fear or no fear.

On finals day, he took his place behind the podium and cleared his throat. "Ladies and gentlemen" he began. "Zaccheus was a very small man—and I've never felt smaller in my life! The second thing I know about Zaccheus was that he was up a tree. And if I was ever up a tree, I'm up one now! But Zaccheus made haste and came down. And that's what I'm going to do right now! Amen."

His message was such a hit it inspired a series, *The One-Minute Minister,* a volume praised by churchgoers everywhere who believe there is no such thing as a bad short sermon!

Zaccheus may have been small and up a tree, both literally and figuratively. But when Jesus Christ passed through the city of Jericho, He stopped to personally invite this hated tax collector to follow Him. So gracious was the invitation that Zaccheus accepted instantly, and as a result, his whole life changed.

Jesus' encounter with this outsider of Jericho has a number of lessons to teach us about how much God cares about those who don't belong.

> And He [Jesus] entered and was passing through Jericho. And behold, there was a man called by the name of Zaccheus; and he was a chief tax-gatherer, and he was rich. And he was trying to see who Jesus was, and he was unable because of the crowd, for he was small in stature. And he ran on ahead and climbed up into a sycamore tree in order to see Him, for He was about to pass through that way. And when Jesus came to the place, He looked up and said to him, "Zaccheus, hurry and come down, for today I must stay at your house." And he hurried and came down, and received Him gladly. And when they saw it, they all began to grumble saying, "He has gone to be the guest of a man who is a sinner." And Zaccheus stopped and said to the Lord, "Behold, Lord, half of my possessions I will give to the poor, and if I have defrauded anyone of anything, I will give back four times as much." And Jesus said to him, "Today salvation has come to this house, because he, too, is a son of Abraham. For the Son of Man has come to seek and to save that which was lost" (Luke 19:1-10).

Setting the Stage

The news spread like a prairie fire in late August: Jesus was coming through Jericho! This Miracle-Worker had stirred the ire of the Pharisees and the curiosity of the common folk for three years now. At last the inhabitants of Jericho would see Him for themselves. Would He do wonders in their midst? Would He feed the town with free bread and the best wine? Might the dead be brought to life? Was He going to walk on water, as He had before? Speculations sizzled and rumor ran rampant.

Earlier inhabitants of Jericho had participated in the miraculous. Fifteen hundred years before, this city had provided the setting for one of God's most dramatic interventions on behalf of His people.

After Joshua and the Children of Israel crossed the Jordan River to enter the Promised Land, capturing Jericho faced them as their first challenge. But instead of a traditional siege, God instructed His people to march around the city for seven days. On the seventh day, they were to blow their trumpets, and the city would be theirs. Sure enough, as the old song retells it, "Joshua fit the battle of Jericho, and the walls came a-tumblin' down." Israel destroyed the city's pagan inhabitants, ransacked their belongings, and claimed its first victory in the land of promise.

Only one family of Jericho escaped annihilation, that of Rahab the harlot. Because she protected Israeli spies, God saved her and her family from destruction.

Now 1,500 years later, God once again offered salvation to an unlikely prospect. This time it was offered to Zaccheus, the tax collector. As Jesus walked through the city, He spied the little man perched above Him, looking down from the limb of a sycamore tree. As He came near, Jesus stopped and looked straight into Zaccheus' eyes and issued a call. "Zaccheus, hurry and come down," He directed, "for today I must stay at your house." The squatty man joyfully scrambled down from the tree and gave Jesus not just his hospitality but his life as well.

The Call Is All-inclusive

Christ excludes no one from His invitation to life. He says, "Let him that is athirst come. And whosoever will, let him take the water of life freely" (Rev. 22:17, KJV).

Our sinfulness can't disqualify us from responding to Christ's call. If it could, surely Zaccheus would have been left out. Judean tax collectors weren't simply first-century IRS agents. They were usually extortionists who milked all the advantage they could from their privileged position with the ruling Roman government. And the Romans planned the system to work this way. To become a tax collector, a Jew would agree to pay the Romans a specific amount of revenue from his district every year. Whatever he took in above that amount was his to keep, so, naturally, fraud abounded. We tease our doctor that his insistence on gall bladder surgery might have been motivated by an impending balloon payment due on his Aspen ski condo. But in the case of many Jewish tax collectors, this would have been no joke. When their needs—or wants—increased, so did the taxes they levied.

Cheating his countrymen to make himself rich would have brought God's disapproval on the tax collector. But even worse, many of the tax men accepted bribes from the wealthy and then "rearranged" the tax burden, so the rich paid little while the poor staggered under the bulk of the taxations.

Yet a tax collector's sinfulness didn't exclude him from Jesus' call. God's call to conversion goes out to all of us, the most sinful included. And indeed, the ones we judge most undeserving may be the prime candidates for true conversion because they understand their need.

A few years ago, our church conducted a neighborhood survey to find out more about the people around us we might be reaching. In the process, we collected information on more than 2,000 households near our church. Of course, we knew we couldn't effectively meet the needs of so many, so I met with church leaders to try to decide which families we'd focus on.

"Let's take these response cards we've received, and sort them into two piles," I suggested. "One pile we'll call 'prospects,' those people we think will be responsive to the Gospel. The other pile will be 'suspects,' those we suspect won't be as interested in what we have to offer." The church officials agreed to this plan, and we began to read the cards one by one.

What I didn't tell them was that before the meeting, I had stacked the deck. I inserted cards that described the three families that had most recently joined our church but disguised their names so the church officials wouldn't recognize them.

The card for one of these families came up first, and I read the information. "This family has a father, thirty-eight years old, a mother, thirty-five, and two children, ages five and eleven." Then I read the family's past religious affiliation with a church we'd consider highly unbiblical. When I announced the church's name, one man said firmly, "They'd never be open to help from us!" So I took the card, tore it in half, and threw it in the trash.

Another family newly joined to our congregation showed up on the next card. Without reading their name, I described their past religious leanings and life circumstances. "They'd never want to be part of our church family either," someone responded immediately. So again, I tore the card in half and tossed it in the wastebasket.

The third card described a third family new to our church, and again this family was dubbed "impossible" and the card was destroyed.

My moment had come. "Before we go on," I said quietly, "I'd like to backtrack and tell you the names of the three families that we've just written off."

I fished out the remains of their cards and, to the group's embarrassment, named people *already* a part of our fellowship!

How easy it is to assume we—or others around us—are too sinful to be candidates for grace. Fortunately, Jesus makes no such distinctions because His call is inclusive.

The New Testament shows God offering forgiveness to thieves, liars, adulterers, murderers, and hypocrites—even to those used by Satan to crucify God's Son. All are invited alike. In almost thirty years of preaching, I've seen people come to Christ from nearly every background imaginable. At the close of one service, a ten-year-old boy walked down one aisle to commit himself to Christ, a seventy-five-year-old man came down the other aisle to make the same decision, and both came away equally cleansed. God sets no limits on how much sin He will forgive. When Jesus called Zaccheus, He invited a blatant sinner to share in God's life. We needn't scrub up or shape up or shore up before He opens His arms to us. His call is an inclusive call.

Christ's Call Is Personal

When Jesus came to Jericho, He didn't shout, "Hey! Everyone without God! Come to Me." He didn't send out a bulk mailing with the Gospel enclosed to the whole zip code area. Instead, He singled out one little man in a tree and said, "Zaccheus, come." Though God wants all to belong to Him, He invites us one at a time. God's call comes more often through a telephone than it does a microphone.

Back in 1976, when Billy Graham came to St. Louis, his associate Grady Wilson preached at my church. As we visited informally, I mentioned that even though I'd pastored a church in Minneapolis, where the Graham organization is headquartered, and I had worked for a year for the Billy Graham Evangelistic Association, I'd never met Dr. Graham personally.

Grady Wilson decided that oversight needed to be remedied at once, so he set up a meeting for me with Dr. Graham at 2:00 that afternoon.

Finally getting to talk with the man I'd chosen as a model for my evangelistic work made me so nervous I had butterfly salad for lunch. And the security precautions surrounding the evangelist didn't do much to allay my anxiety. The meeting instructions I was given sounded like they were created by an ex-spy novelist. Go to a certain gate of the arena where Dr. Graham was preaching, I was told, and wait for a black limousine to drive up. Three men would get out of the car and enter a door just across from where I stood. "Do not move, do not wave, do not speak," my contact said. "Just stand still and wait." In about five minutes, someone would appear at the door and motion for me to enter.

The car arrived, just as I expected, and the three men got out and disappeared through the door. As I waited, it felt like five hours instead of five minutes dragged by as I shifted from one foot to the other and nervously rehearsed what I was going to say. Finally, the signal came. I gulped and apprehensively entered the room.

There sat Billy Graham on the couch in front of me. When he saw me, he stood, walked toward me with his hand extended, and exclaimed, "Bob! I have heard so much about you and Donna and the great job you are doing at First Baptist!"

At that moment my tension vanished. Dr. Graham called me by name! His personal interest in me dispelled my fear.

So it is with God. He knows us personally, calls us individually, and works through us one by one.

Some of us learn that lesson more quickly than others.

A nervous mother in New Haven, Connecticut rushed in to see her pastor one day.

"I just don't know what to do with my little boy," she flustered. "I overheard him saying his prayers the other night, and he prayed, 'Our Father, who art in New Haven, how in the world did You know my name?' ''

"Madam," the pastor replied, "I recommend you don't do a single thing, because your son's prayer shows he has grasped two great truths. He believes that God knows his address and that He knows him by name."

When God chose to populate the earth, He worked through individuals, a man named Adam and a woman named Eve. Later, when wickedness reigned in the world, He dealt with Noah to save humanity. Then followed Abraham, Sarah, Jacob, Joseph, Moses, Joshua, Deborah, David, Esther, and others— all individuals whom God knew by name.

And as the New Testament opens, God again demonstrates His involvement with individuals. To prepare the way for the Messiah, "there came *a man,* sent from God, whose *name was John*" (John 1:6, emphasis added). Not a delegation sent from God, but one man. And not just any man. God knew this servant personally; his name was John.

Though Jesus preached to multitudes, much of the Gospel story centers on His personal encounters—here with a mother whose child was ill, there with a man who could not see. And His leadership training program was offered to twelve individuals whom Jesus called by name. That's why it's entirely acceptable to take John 3:16 and make it your own. Instead of saying "God so loved the world, that He gave His only begotten Son, that whoever believes in Him should not perish," I can rightly say, "For God so loved Bob Werner, that He gave His only begotten Son, that if Bob Werner would believe in Him, he will not perish, but have eternal life." Jesus calls us individually, as He did Zaccheus.

We must answer His call individually as well. God has no grandchildren, only children. Parents can't decide if their children will respond to Him. Husbands can't decide for their wives, nor wives for their husbands. Christ calls each of us personally, and each of us must respond.

Christ's Call Is Urgent

"Zaccheus, *hurry* and come down."

Jesus' call had an element of urgency to it. Though God is always ready to receive us, there are moments when we stand more ready to receive Him than others. What we decide in those moments can determine our destiny.

Several years ago a husband and his wife in Jefferson City, Missouri were driving to work one morning when their car stalled. The man got out to investigate the trouble, and as he did, he absentmindedly stuck a cigarette in his mouth and reached for his lighter. But he didn't know a gas pipe located near the highway had sprung a leak in the night, filling the low spot where their car was parked with natural gas. When the man flicked his lighter, he touched off a massive explosion. Though the car shielded him from the worst of the blast, his wife took the full impact and was burned from head to foot.

I was called to her bedside in the hospital's burn unit a few hours later. The woman could not speak; she could manage only to nod her head.

"Are you a Christian?" I asked her. She shook her head negatively.

"Would you like to become one?" I went on. She nodded a yes.

"If I take the Scriptures and share with you how to become a Christian, can you hear me?" I asked, and she nodded that she could. I shared the Gospel, and when I asked if she'd like to invite Christ to take her life, she not only nodded a yes, but tears welled up in her eyes.

From the time of the accident until I reached the hospital, this woman had been unconscious. And an hour after I spoke with her, she lapsed into a coma and died the next day. God's call to her would not come again. Had she decided, "I'll think about God after I'm through the worst of this," the window of opportunity would have closed before her, and her eternal destiny would have been sealed without God.

To this woman, the urgency of the call was evident. But sometimes only God knows how urgent it is that we say yes to His call. When Zaccheus encountered Jesus, the Lord was headed for Jerusalem. He would never pass through Jericho again, for within a matter of days, He would end His earthly life at the cross. If Zaccheus had thought, *Maybe next time I see Him I'll consider His claims more seriously,* he'd have missed eternal life because there would be no next time. Zaccheus didn't know this would be his last opportunity with Jesus, but Jesus knew, and thus His call to the tax collector was tinged with urgency.

Bruce Thielemann, pastor of the First Presbyterian Church of Pittsburgh, says this about God's urgent call: " 'Tomorrow' is the word the Bible does not know. The Holy Spirit's word is *today.* 'Now is the accepted time.' 'Now is the day of salvation.' 'Today if you will harden not your hearts and hear my voice.' Don't say tomorrow!"

He goes on to recount a fable of Satan's search for a demonic messenger to send to earth who would lure men and women toward the destruction of their souls. He asked for volunteers.

One stepped forward. "I'll tell them there is no heaven," he offered. But Satan knew this message wouldn't have effect because in every person lives the sense that right must prevail and be rewarded.

Another, more evil than the first, stepped forward. "I'll say there is no hell," he asserted. But Satan rejected him because the human conscience assures each one that evil must one day be punished.

Then the last demonic messenger stepped forward. "I can assure humanity's destruction," he told his master, "for I will tell them that there is no hurry."

Satan said, "Go" (Bruce Thielemann, "Claiming the Molten Moment," *Christianity Today,* February 1, 1985, pp. 30–31).

Christ's Call Is Transforming

Sometimes I meet people who resist becoming Christians because they feel they can't live up to the challenge. But the wonderful truth is that they don't have to! All they must do is give God permission to transform them, and He does the living through them. If they could do it without Him, there'd be no need for conversion.

Zaccheus responded to the Lord's call and was changed. This man who'd made his livelihood by fraud and deception announced, "Half of my possessions I will give to the poor, and if I have defrauded anyone of anything, I will give back four times as much." There's no record of Jesus making this demand on the tax collector. Genuine conversion had made him new from the inside out, and his actions showed it. He had freely received life from Jesus; it seemed natural now to freely give.

Can you imagine Zaccheus going back to a little old lady from whom he had wrongfully taken money?

He knocks on her door. A small voice from inside calls, "Who's there?"

"It's me, Zaccheus."

"Please," the woman inside begins to plead. "Zaccheus, you took all I had when you were here last week. I have no more to give you. I'm just a poor widow. Please."

"You don't understand," Zaccheus interrupts her. "I'm not here to take money from you. I came to give you money."

The woman is sure now she must either be hallucinating or the victim of a hoax. She hurries to the door and cracks it just enough to see what trickster would play this cruel joke. But it really is Zaccheus. Or at least it looks like Zaccheus. Same man, same clothes, same small stature, yet somehow he looks strangely different. Could it be the look of kindness on his face that seems so out of place?

She pushes the door open. "Zaccheus, is it really you?"

He smiles and reaches for her hand. Into it he presses a pouch of money, closing her fingers over it. "I've been unfair to you," he says slowly. "I took more than my due, so you'll find I have compensated you four times over for everything I took wrongfully. I'm sorry." And he turns to go.

The old woman stands motionless for a moment, stunned with surprise. But then she reaches out after him. "Zaccheus," she calls. "What has happened to you?"

Zaccheus turns back and stands as tall as his small stature will allow, and with laughter in his eyes, he replies, "Madam, Jesus happened to me!"

Responding to Jesus' call transforms us. It doesn't reform us or simply spruce up what we were before. We're changed by Him into someone entirely new.

The changes can be as dramatic as they were with Zaccheus, or they can be more gradual. A few years ago, a crippled farmer in his seventies invited me into his two-room shack so he could tell me of his conversion. "It happened when I was fifty-seven," he began. "Up to that time, I was the meanest, orneriest cuss around. Nobody liked me. I mistreated my wife. My dogs were afraid of me. My milk cows would hardly let me touch them. Even my machinery was all broke down because I abused it so bad."

But then the local Baptist church held a revival. "I went on a dare more than anything else," the old man confessed. "When I walked into the church, you could about hear the eyeballs pop open as the people saw me come in. I knew they were thinking, 'E.B. Halley is here?'

"I don't know how to explain it," he went on, "but the only

thing I know to tell you is that I gave my heart to Jesus that night. And this will be the hard part for you to believe," he hesitated as his eyes twinkled. "The next day, my cows would let me milk them! It was almost as though they knew that I had been converted."

This change was the beginning of many, much more significant changes in E.B. Halley. The meanest cuss in the community became a kind and caring husband and neighbor, all because responding to God's call transforms outsiders. Mr. Halley, like Zaccheus, is now a member of God's family.

CHAPTER TWO
Lydia—The Seeker

When *Christianity Today* magazine ran a special study of the changing role of women, the cover illustration painted a graphic portrait of the new woman of the eighties. On the wall of a home hung a painting in which a woman, sedately settled in her rocker, passively rocked away her life. But beneath the painting sat today's woman, dressed for success in a black suit, white blouse, and obligatory paisley bow tie. And her hands weren't passively folded in her lap; this woman's fingers were poised above a portable computer keyboard. And instead of using a footstool, she rested her Adidas-clad feet on a pile of *Wall Street Journals*.

In Acts 16, Scripture introduces us to a woman who would have perhaps been more comfortable here in the 1980s than she was in her own day. Lydia of Philippi was a successful businesswoman, perhaps even an entrepreneur, who experienced the miracle of conversion. How she did it holds lessons for today's businesswomen—and businessmen—as well.

And on the Sabbath day we went outside the gate to a riverside, where we were supposing that there would be a place of prayer; and we sat down and began speaking to the women who had assembled. And a certain woman named Lydia, from the city of Thyatira, a seller of purple fabrics, a worshiper of God, was listening; and the Lord opened her heart to respond to the things spoken by Paul. And when she and her household had been baptized, she urged us, saying, "If you have judged me to be faithful to the Lord, come into my house and stay." And she prevailed upon us (Acts 16:13-15).

Setting the Stage

Paul had set off on his second missionary journey, taking Silas and Timothy with him. They proceeded according to plan, visiting churches Paul had planted on his first missionary trek. But then the Holy Spirit forbade them to preach the Gospel in Asia. I can imagine the frustration Paul must have felt at this holy intervention. He had a mandate to preach yet sensed God not allowing him to do so. Was God saying yes or no? But the confusion lifted in Troas when Paul received a vision of a man in Macedonia (our modern-day Europe) pleading, "Come over to Macedonia and help us." Dr. Luke had joined the little troop by this time, so the four men caught a boat for Macedonia and settled in Philippi, described in Scripture as "a leading city of Macedonia."

Now what? In cities where they'd preached before, they started at the Jewish synagogue, but Philippi was a Roman colony, and no such synagogue existed. Were they supposed to wait for the man in the vision to find them? How were they to begin to reach this city with the Gospel? They stayed in the city "for some days," Luke records, but by the Sabbath they'd waited long enough. There might be no synagogue, but they'd heard of a prayer meeting by the river outside the city. Perhaps there they'd learn what their next step was to be.

At the riverside prayer meeting, Paul may have been disappointed when he didn't spot the man in the vision. Instead, he found a group of women, one of whom was to become the central figure in the founding of the first Christian church in Europe. The woman's name was Lydia.

As we've said, Lydia appears to have been a successful and gracious businesswoman. When Luke describes her as "a seller of purple," he's telling us that Lydia knew the Roman business climate and worked it to her advantage. You see, the "purple" Lydia peddled was purple-dyed fabrics. Her hometown, the city of Thyatira, was an area well known in the Roman world for its purple dyes, produced from the murex shellfish, a type of Mediterranean snail. Perhaps Lydia learned the textile trade working in her father's or her husband's business; we're not told. No mention is made of her husband, so perhaps she never married or was widowed. In any case, Luke speaks of "her" household.

But carrying on a textile trade in Philippi showed good sense because Philippi was a Roman colony and therefore subject to Roman regulation and customs. The Romans had declared purple the color of royalty and therefore to be worn by all citizens at certain times of the year. To own a purple-fabric franchise in this city could have been as lucrative as owning an Orange Crush outlet in a city full of Denver Bronco fans.

Lydia also seems to have been a strong leader. When she received the Gospel, her household was baptized with her. There appears to have been no dallying over making a decision. And she graciously invited Paul and the others to be guests in her home, but her invitation was hardly passive. "If you have judged me to be faithful to the Lord," she entreated them, "come into my house and stay." If they had refused, they would have been judging her unfaithful. How could these preachers refuse such an invitation? And Luke goes on to say, "She prevailed upon us." How many people in the Scripture ever managed to "prevail" upon the strong-minded Apostle Paul? Yet Lydia decided he and his party would stay at her home, and stay they did.

During their stay, her home became the center for a company of believers. After Paul and Silas did time in the Philippian prison, they went back to Lydia's home, "and when they saw the brethren, they encouraged them and departed" (Acts 16:40). Lydia's natural leadership and aggressive hospitality made her a key player in the drama of taking the Gospel to the world.

Lydia's conversion wasn't very dramatic. Zaccheus, you remember, underwent an instantaneous transformation from scoundrel to generous benefactor. Surely the entire town buzzed with news of the change in him. Was Lydia's conversion less real? Of course not! Her life bore the fruit of a spirit genuinely rooted in Christ. Her conversion came more quietly, but it did come, and she has some things to teach us about what happens when a creative, aggressive individual connects with Christ.

Lydia Was Religious without Being Converted

When Lydia met Paul, she had gathered with other women to pray to the God of Israel. Somewhere along the line, this Gentile woman had encountered Judaism and chosen to believe it was true. But she had also chosen to practice her beliefs in a climate where she lacked encouragement. Jewish law said that in a city where at least ten Jewish males age twelve or older resided, a synagogue must be built. But Philippi had no such synagogue, so Jews must have been a rarity. This handful of women gathered at the river may have been the only believers in the city. For a Gentile businesswoman to worship openly as part of such a distinct religious minority took great courage. Lydia was a genuinely religious woman, yet Scripture makes it clear she was not yet converted.

Just because we behave like people who've been converted doesn't guarantee the new birth has actually taken place. My $49.95 fake Rolex may appear identical to your genuine $4,995 watch. Our watches may impress our friends as being equally authentic. But when we try to sell them, the difference in the checks we receive will reveal which watch was the genuine Rolex.

So it is with some of us. Our religious behavior can make us look like real Christians, yet we're not. One of the greatest lessons I've ever learned about human nature is this: you can act like a Christian without being one, and you can be a Christian without acting like one.

Lydia prayed, but she was not yet converted. I prayed often before I was converted. Sometimes I prayed from a sense of responsibility, other times to alleviate guilt. Most often, I prayed when I got in trouble. I pulled out one of those prayers that began, "Lord, if you get me out of this mess, I promise I'll. . . ." Lydia not only prayed, she joined with others for worship, even when it wasn't the popular or convenient thing to do. She came to worship, but she wasn't converted. Prayer and gathering for worship are things Christians do, but doing them doesn't make us Christians. Even a belief in God doesn't make us Christians. The Apostle James said, "You believe that God is one. . . . the *demons* also believe, and shudder" (James 2:19, emphasis added).

Lydia Sought the Lord Until He Found Her

Some people use piety as a shield behind which they hide to protect themselves from having to confront Christ Himself. They use religious appearances as an inoculation to help them build immunity, so they'll never "catch" the disease of Christianity in its full force. For these people, religion can be the greatest enemy Jesus Christ has. But for others, like Lydia, religion is no cop-out. Prayer and worship became stepping-stones to a personal encounter with God because Lydia was seeking the Lord. While Paul spoke, she listened. "She attended unto the things which were spoken of Paul" (Acts 16:14, KJV). This woman wasn't sitting in church, hoping the message would get over soon so she could get to the restaurant before the Methodists took all the best tables. She was listening, seeking the Lord. In Jeremiah 29:13, the Lord promises, "And you will seek Me and find Me, when you search for Me with all your heart." Lydia found the Lord because she sought Him.

People all around us are seeking the Lord, just as Lydia was. Peter instructs those of us who want to help them in their search: "Sanctify the Lord God in your hearts: and be ready always to give an answer to every man that asketh you a reason of the hope that is in you with meekness and fear" (1 Peter 3:15, KJV). It's not up to us to push these seekers into Christ's life, yet there are ways we can help them.

First, we can reverence Christ as Lord in our own hearts. As we love and worship Him, we'll quite naturally be known as His followers. Seekers after Him will know they can come to us as guides. If you wanted to know more about last year's quarterback for the Dolphins, who would you ask? Doesn't some sports fanatic you know come immediately to mind? Sports fans are known for their passion! They don't need to buy advertising space to let others know of their sports commitment. We know them because they're never in church on Superbowl Sunday, they have their own subscriptions to *Sporting News,* they show up for committee meetings in jogging suits, and they're forever trying to sell us candy bars or Christmas wreaths because they're raising money to buy new uniforms for the Babe Ruth teams. If you have a passion, those around you will know. And when we're reverencing Christ as our Lord, that passion will show as well.

Second, we can be ready to answer the questions of those seeking Christ. Unfortunately, not many who are seeking Christ seem to come right out and say so. How often have you had an unbeliever approach you and say, "I've heard you're a Christian. I'm not, but I'd like to be. Could you show me how?" If you are like me, this has seldom happened to you. But that doesn't mean non-Christians aren't seeking. It means their seeking is a bit more subtle, and we need to learn to recognize their questions when they don't come quite so directly.

For instance, because Lydia was seeking the Lord, she converted from a pagan religion to Judaism. Do you know anyone who is exploring some new system of religion? Or do you know anyone who comes to church, even though they don't seem to know Christ? They may be telling you they are seeking the Lord, just as Lydia was. Sometimes people seek Christ by casually taking the initiative toward us. One woman said, "A woman I barely knew invited me to play tennis on a regular basis. As we got to know each other better, I realized she was hungry for Christ and knew of my faith before we began meeting for tennis. I think she took the initiative because she wanted an up-close look at the faith, but to approach a minister, or even me, directly with her questions would have been too threatening. She feared being pushed but wanted to find out about Christ on her own timetable. Our weekly meetings gave her a chance to poke at me from a variety of angles before she trusted me enough to talk about her real concerns."

This seeker disguised herself as a tennis partner. Others come in the form of office mates who insist on telling you about their Uncle Eddy getting religion. Some seekers couch their curiosity in grousing over hypocrites in the church or television ministers who go astray. They complain to you because it's their way of bringing up spiritual issues in a way that protects them from commitments they're not ready to make. May God open our eyes and ears to the seekers around us, so we can respond to their probes in a way that points them toward Christ.

The responses we give don't need to be authoritarian. Peter only requires that we respond "with meekness and fear" (1 Peter 3:15, KJV). Meek responses are gentle and open. Instead of closing the door on a conversation, they leave room for further discussion. We often confuse good answers with debate clinchers. We picture ourselves coming up with such an astounding and attack-proof answer to a seeker's question that he will be awestruck into the kingdom.

But Scripture presents a different picture of God's wisdom. "The wisdom from above is first pure, then peaceable, gentle, reasonable, full of mercy" (James 3:17). Real wisdom is willing to respond honestly but also willing to listen to *all* the questioner's concerns. So if you feel you're too fearful or too unsure you'll be able to offer perfect help to a seeker, relax. Meekness and fear are advantages here, because you're not in this alone. As you direct others to Christ, the Lord Himself becomes your partner in witnessing to the truth.

As Lydia sought the Lord, God opened her heart to the truth. Conversion is a supernatural visitation. Though human beings can carry the message of conversion, true conversion is a mysterious and divine transaction that can't be manipulated or cajoled or emoted into being.

One day a drunken man approached Billy Graham and stuck out his hand toward the great evangelist. "Shake hands, Billy," the man said. "I'm one of your converts."

Billy Graham looked at him and said, "You are one of my converts, I'm sure, because if you were one of His, you wouldn't be in the condition you are in."

God opened Lydia's heart, and He does this for all who come to Him. We don't have to pry others' hearts open to conversion. All we have to do is point the way as they seek. The Lord will find them.

Lydia Confirmed Her Faith in Baptism

Lydia and her household were baptized as their first act of obedience to Christ. By this act, Lydia confirmed to all who knew her that she was now a follower of the Lord and part of the company of those who identified with Him.

Did Lydia have to be baptized to go to heaven? The answer is no because baptism doesn't qualify anyone for heaven. In a few chapters we'll investigate the conversion of a dying thief who came to faith in Jesus. If baptism is a necessity to enter God's kingdom, Jesus would have been wrong to promise this thief eternal life, because the thief died on a Roman cross with no chance to be baptized.

But baptism is commanded both by Christ and the apostles as an outward act symbolizing an inward change. And Christ Himself gave us an example when He chose to be baptized by John the Baptist. This pattern of following a conversion experience with baptism is repeated throughout the New Testament.

Not everyone shares my enthusiasm for baptism. Some worry that if we encourage new Christians to be baptized, they'll think that baptism is somehow necessary to complete their salvation.

Of course, that's a ridiculous and unbiblical notion. Baptism isn't important because of what it *does;* it's important because of what it *shows.* In Romans 6, Paul makes it clear that when we believe in Jesus, we die to our lives of sin and come to new life by God's power. We're not just sinners saved by grace; we're now *saints!* We'll probably be sinning saints, given the temptation in the world around us and the weakness of our human flesh, but we're saints nonetheless.

The physical act the Lord provided to picture this new life is baptism, and what could symbolize it better? We're "buried" to our old life and raised again by a power beyond us. The Lord provided this act of baptism as a tactile, visible way to witness to the invisible, mysterious miracle that's taken place in our spirit.

If you poked in my wallet, you'd find a photo of my beautiful, six-year-old granddaughter. And if you tried to remove it, you'd hear Grandpa putting up a fuss because I value that picture. Why? Is it because I believe the picture *is* my granddaughter? Do I think that losing that picture will mean losing my granddaughter? Of course not. The photo does nothing more than portray her. If I didn't have the photo, she'd still be just as real.

But her picture reminds me of her. And it gives me a tangible way to share the delight she brings me with others.

So it is with baptism. Dunking in a pool of water won't convert you; nor will it "complete" your conversion. But it does portray what happened at conversion and therefore gives us a deeply meaningful way to witness to God, ourselves, and others that we've begun a brand-new life.

Lydia Took Her Conversion Home with Her

When Lydia converted to Christianity, her household also converted. And her first "ministry" as a new believer was insisting that Paul, Luke, and the others with them come home with her. Christianity was never meant to be left at the church; it was meant to invade our homes, our workplaces, our relaxation, and our friendships. Jesus is called "Emmanuel," *God with us.* Our bodies become His dwelling place, so where we go, He goes.

During the initial stages of His public ministry, Christ met a demon-possessed man in Gerasenes and healed him. Before his encounter with Christ, the man's life had been ruined by what we'd define as mental illness. In the past, people in his town had tried to subdue him with chains and shackles, but he broke them all and now lived alone among the tombs of a graveyard, crying and cutting himself with stones. Christ transformed the man into someone who was "sitting down, clothed and in his right mind" (Mark 5:15). As Jesus turned to leave, the man begged to accompany Him, but Jesus said no. "Go home to your people," Christ instructed him, "and report to them what great things the Lord has done for you, and how He had mercy on you" (Mark 5:19).

When Christ claims us, He sends us home to live out the faith with the people who know us best. And because He indwells us, He goes with us to our homes to eat breakfast with us, grocery shop with us, watch TV with us, pay bills with us, and discipline our kids with us. He comes to live where we live so through us He can give His life and love to those in our world. Real faith was never meant to be enjoyed only in stained-glass buildings from 9:30 to 12:00 on Sunday morning. Our Saviour was a rugged carpenter, not a religious professional. His closest companions were salty fishermen, political revolutionaries, and IRS agents, not priests and Pharisees. He wants to be part of our real life, and when conversion is real, our Mondays through Saturdays become as much His as our Sunday mornings do.

Lydia came to faith and knew at once she wanted to take her Saviour and His followers into her home.

This successful businesswoman sought the Lord, and when He found her, her conversion affected her whole household as well, laying foundation for the birth of a church.

CHAPTER THREE
Ethiopian Eunuch—The Rich and Powerful One

Weddings can take place in some of the strangest places. I've heard of couples entering into holy matrimony while deep-sea diving or parachuting through the clouds. But one of the most unique weddings of the year occurred here in Florida—at a supermarket.

A magazine reporter explained:

They were both tired of shopping for love in meat markets that passed for local singles' spots, so it was especially ironic that when Debbie Francis and Vic Radeka met last October, it was in front of a meat counter at a Publix Supermarket in Davie, Florida during the store's first Singles' Night. And it was especially fitting that, a year later, the couple chose to exchange their wedding vows in Publix, attended by 150 friends and family members and approximately 850 people they'd never seen before, who stopped loading their grocery carts long enough to watch the proceedings.

A white wrought-iron arch was set up between the cash registers and the bakery department. Though the embarrassed father of the bride threatened to attend wearing a grocery bag over his head, he reneged and came in formal garb, so the wedding came off without a hitch. And after cutting a cake provided by the store's bakery, the couple started their married life by filling a grocery cart and wheeling off into bliss (Laurel Tielis, "Attention, Shoppers: Check Out the Wedding Special in Aisle 2!" *People Weekly*, Oct. 26, 1987, pp. 143–45).

The setting may have been unusual, but that didn't make Debbie and Vic any less married. And conversion can happen in unusual places as well and still be genuine. The biblical account of the conversion of an Ethiopian government official who found God on a dusty road proves you don't need stained glass windows to come to new life.

But an angel of the Lord spoke to Philip saying, "Arise and go south to the road that descends from Jerusalem to Gaza." (This is a desert road.) And he arose and went; and behold, there was an Ethiopian eunuch, a court official of Candace, queen of the Ethiopians, who was in charge of all her treasure; and he had come to Jerusalem to worship. And he was returning and sitting in his chariot, and was reading the prophet Isaiah.

And the Spirit said to Philip, "Go up and join this chariot." And when Philip had run up, he heard him reading Isaiah the prophet, and said, "Do you understand what you are reading?" And he said, "Well, how could I, unless someone guides me?" And he invited Philip to come up and sit with him. . . . And Philip opened his mouth, and beginning from this Scripture he preached Jesus to him. And as they went along the road they came to some water; and the eunuch said,

"Look! Water! What prevents me from being baptized?" And Philip said, "If you believe with all your heart, you may." And he answered, and said, "I believe that Jesus Christ is the Son of God." And he ordered the chariot to stop; and they both went down into the water, Philip as well as the eunuch; and he baptized him. And when they came up out of the water, the Spirit of the Lord snatched Philip away; and the eunuch saw him no more, but went on his way rejoicing (Acts 8:26-31, 35-39).

Setting the Stage

The place is a desert highway leading south from Jerusalem toward the city of Gaza, a final stopover before a traveler headed down to Egypt. An ornately decorated chariot leaves a rooster tail of dust behind it as it bumps down the unpaved road. The chariot driver slows his horses, trying to avoid hitting the deepest ruts, but his master fails to notice, engrossed as he is in the scroll he tries to read between the jolts and jars.

Travelers toward Jerusalem who pass the chariot crane their necks for a better look. The owner is obviously wealthy, and look! Isn't that the royal seal of the kingdom of Ethiopia on the front? What is an Ethiopian doing in the city of the Jews? But the Ethiopian looks past them, struggling with the meaning of the scroll.

The man in the chariot was a government official, Scripture tells us. As keeper of the queen's treasure, he may have even been second in importance in the kingdom since the one who controled the money often carried great power. (One envious wag says rich people live by their own Golden Rule: "He who has the gold makes the rules!") At any rate, this man obviously held a position of great importance.

This Ethiopian official on his way home from worship was headed straight into an encounter with God.

The Ethiopian Showed Desire

An Ethiopian worshipping in Jerusalem would be as likely as a Weight Watchers' graduate managing a Baskin-Robbins ice cream store! But somewhere this Ethiopian had come in contact with news of the one true God. The fact that he had journeyed from the African continent to Jerusalem to worship as this God prescribed shows the official was serious in his search for spiritual reality. He wanted to know God, even if it cost him time, money, inconvenience, and discomfort.

He sought the Lord, but the Lord was at the same time seeking him. We aren't told what God had done to cause him to thirst for the water of life. Was there a friend at home or someone at court whose life he had observed? On the Day of Pentecost, both Africans and Arabs heard the Gospel in their native languages. Perhaps God used one of these to take the story back to Ethiopia, so God could begin to draw a certain court official to Himself.

We never know when we'll be part of God's plan to bring someone to conversion. A couple years ago, a Christian woman I know found herself grounded in Chicago's O'Hare Airport by a canceled flight connection. She fumed about the two-hour delay but then realized that the Lord might have engineered it for a purpose.

Indeed, He had. Within a few minutes she found herself sharing a table in a crowded snack bar with an English businessman who declared himself to be an atheist. Yet as they talked, he confided with some embarrassment that he'd been going deaf, but when a Christian friend prayed for him, his hearing had inexplicably improved so markedly that he no longer needed either of his two hearing aids. He'd never before told anyone of the healing because he realized he'd have to credit it to Jesus, and "all my friends laugh at the religious fanatics we know," he said.

The Christian woman shared her faith in Christ, and the two parted cordially. She said later, "What an amazing amount of initiative God was taking toward this man! The Lord had made him aware of the truth through those he called 'fanatics'; He healed the man's deafness; then He provided a 'chance' meeting with a Christian in America to confirm again Christ's reality. My friend later wrote to him, 'I don't know if you are seeking Christ, but it seems apparent that He's seeking you!' "

When God's drawing and our response come together, conversion happens, just as it did for the Ethiopian.

The Ethiopian Had a Direction to Follow

When Philip met him, the Ethiopian ruler was reading the Bible. To know the way back to Ethiopia, his driver likely needed a road map to follow. And in his spiritual journey, the Ethiopian needed a road map as well, so he wisely turned to the Bible.

The Bible isn't a book of science to show us how the heavens go. Rather, it's a book to tell us how to go to heaven. And what an excellent resource it is!

In Psalm 119, David devotes his longest psalm to extolling the glories of God's Word, and there he offers some interesting perspectives on God's Word as our road map.

He tells the Lord, "Thy word is a lamp to my feet, and a light to my path" (Ps. 119:105). We get on God's path by choosing to follow what God has said, David tells us. "Remove the false way from me," David pleads to the Lord, ". . . [for] I have chosen the faithful way; I have placed Thine ordinances before me" (Ps. 119:29-30).

David realized a choice of life maps lay before him. Many would prove false; one, faithful. Which map he'd use to guide him was his choice to make, and he chose God's Word. With this guide, he began to walk in God's way, and the Scriptures provided the light he needed.

One caution needs to be offered here, however. When David said the Scriptures served as a lamp to his feet, he had a special picture in mind. In Bible times, roadways weren't brightly illuminated for miles ahead by megawattage street-lights. To find their way, travelers carried oil lamps, either in their hands or attached to their feet. Thus each step might be clearly illumined, but only as the step was taken. To find out what lay a mile up ahead, the traveler had to walk there, one lighted step at a time.

We sometimes mistakenly think God operates like a motor club. We tell AAA we want to go from Sarasota to Seattle, and they send a completed chart for the entire journey. Before we pack the cartop carrier in Florida, we can know exactly what road we'll be taking each day until arrival.

But God's road map doesn't work that way. It functions more like the directions in a kids' computer game called "Treasure Trek." In this adventure, the end of the journey is clear: you're going to find the treasure. All the directions you need to make your way through a maze of tunnels and obstacles toward the treasure are provided. But they're not handed out before you start the game; they're revealed a step at a time.

When the game begins, you enter a computer-generated cave. But as you journey farther inside, you're faced with choices. A side tunnel emerges on your left. Should you take it or walk on by? The game offers clues to help you make the right choice, but the journey doesn't progress until *you* type in your decision. Sometimes a wrong choice leads to danger or a dead end, so it's necessary to retrace your steps and choose a different way. Guidance only comes a screen at a time.

Sometimes I've wished God would show me all the consequences of my choices at once. Sometimes I long to know what next month, or next year, or the next decade holds in store. But God promises no such light. He offers us only direction enough to safely take the step right before us.

But at the same time, He provides more than any silly computer game ever could. He promises to lead us in our choices ("I will instruct you and teach you in the way which you should go"—Ps. 32:8). And He promises to be with us in each step of the journey ("He Himself has said, 'I will never desert you, nor will I ever forsake you' "—Heb. 13:5). The Ethiopian chose well when he looked to God's Word as his direction for life.

The Ethiopian read Isaiah and found Jesus. He's there, of course, and in every other book from Genesis to Revelation as well. Christ told the Pharisees, "You search the Scriptures, because you think that in them you have eternal life; and it is these that bear witness of *Me*" (John 5:39, emphasis added).

The Jewish religious leaders saw the Bible as a book of rules and life precepts, yet they missed its real purpose. The Scriptures present a sixty-six-act drama about the life and mission of Christ. The Pharisees spent their time arguing over the stage settings and wrangling about appropriate dialogue for the drama but missed the central character altogether.

The Ethiopian Had a Director

For some of us, even the best maps require explanation. So it was with the Ethiopian. He had God's Word to direct him, but he needed a guide to help him understand the truth. That God-sent guide was Philip.

The first mention of Philip is in Acts 6, when a dispute arose in the early church. It seems the Greek converts believed their widows were being discriminated against in the daily food distributions, so the apostles appointed seven men to oversee this part of the church's common life. The seven were to be "men of good reputation, full of the Spirit and of wisdom" (Acts 6:3).

One of the men chosen, Philip, proved to have these strengths and more besides. Two chapters later, in Acts 8, Philip shows up in Samaria after a massive persecution forced believers to leave Jerusalem. In Samaria, Philip began preaching the Gospel, healing, and casting out demons. He stirred up such a revival that Peter and John came from Jerusalem to help in the harvest of new believers.

But in the middle of such great success, the Lord told Philip to leave and head for the desert road that ran between Jerusalem and Gaza. Scripture records simply, "He arose and went" (Acts 8:27). In the midst of excitement and noise and activity and productive ministry, Philip heard the Lord calling him to leave. And when he heard the call, he didn't balk or argue or pout. At this point, Philip didn't know why he was to leave or where his journey might end. But he didn't insist on answers to these questions before he gave notice to the revival committee; he simply went. Would we have done as much?

When Philip saw the Ethiopian's chariot, the Spirit told him to go up and join it. Once again, Philip simply did as he was told. I could have thought of a number of reasons not to do as Philip did. For one thing, what might the Ethiopian think of his approach? We fear for our safety today when we pick up hitchhikers, but travelers on Judean desert roads had just as much reason for apprehension. Robbers regularly attacked travelers. (The road between Jerusalem and Jericho proved to be so dangerous it was unofficially dubbed "the red and bloody way" by some.) Would the chariot driver suspect him of foul play as he approached the vehicle?

And what assurance did Philip have of even being able to communicate with the occupant of the chariot? They might not even speak the same language. He'd certainly have to confront a racial and cultural barrier. Philip wasn't a man of wealth. Would he be comfortable with the monied and powerful Ethiopian ruler? Would he know proper protocol?

All these "what-ifs" might have kept some of us from approaching the chariot, but not Philip. The Spirit said "Go," and he went, trusting God to supply what he needed.

How wonderful that he did because the Lord provided a perfect introduction. Philip heard the Ethiopian reading from Isaiah, and a gracious opening popped into his mind. "Do you understand what you are reading?" he asked the ruler. "How could I," the man replied, "unless someone guides me?" And he invited Philip to join him. Philip took the passage before them, and led the Ethiopian to conversion.

When God readies a person for new birth, He most often uses people as His tool, just as He used Philip to guide the Ethiopian to Christ.

The Ethiopian Had a Decision to Make

After hearing the Gospel, the Ethiopian saw a pond or stream and asked to be baptized. "If you believe with all your heart, you may," Philip wisely counseled him. And the Ethiopian affirmed, "I believe that Jesus Christ is the Son of God." The chariot rumbled to a halt, and the new convert waded into the water.

Just getting information about the Lord wasn't enough for this Ethiopian. He needed to commit himself to the truth of the Gospel and show his commitment in a public identification with Christ. His decision may have come quickly, but it may not have come easily. Would he lose his job as a result of his new faith? Would he become an outsider among the rich and powerful Ethiopians with whom he associated? What would his family think? Perhaps he weighed some of these considerations as he contemplated the claims of Christ, counting what it might cost him.

Following Christ always means leaving something behind in order to take hold of something better up ahead. Jesus put it this way: "The kingdom of heaven is like a treasure hidden in the field, which a man found and hid; and from joy over it he goes and sells all that he has, and buys that field" (Matt. 13:44). Perhaps his decision seemed silly to others; maybe some days it even seemed silly to him, to risk the known for the unknown. But in return, he gained something of great value. And the treasure we receive is nothing less than eternal life.

But nothing of great value comes without cost. And we can't receive the treasure without agreeing to pay the price, abandoning our right to control our own lives, and offering ourselves to Christ's control. The treasure doesn't come to us automatically; it becomes ours only as we *decide* we want it.

The Ethiopian Demonstrated Delight

When Philip and the Ethiopian ruler came up out of the water, the Spirit snatched Philip away. The Ethiopian would not see him again and went on his way. Was he as sad as a man who just discovered someone shot his hound dog? No! He went away *rejoicing!*

Emotion and conversion have a unique relationship. Feelings don't produce conversion, but conversion nearly always results in new feelings. When Peter and John healed the lame man by the temple gate, the man entered the temple walking and leaping and praising God. His joy exploded.

Such expressions are to be expected. Do you remember the birth of your first child? I'll bet it was marked by banners and balloons and outrageous long-distance bills because you called all your relatives. The advent of new life gives us cause for excitement, and so it is with conversion.

But these jubilant feelings needn't accompany conversion for it to be real. I've heard it said that spiritual reality isn't measured by how loud a man shouts but rather by how straight he walks when he hits the ground again. In this sense, conversion becomes much like marriage. Loving another person often generates unspeakable joy. People in love laugh and dance and sing for reasons even they don't understand.

But it's completely possible to love deeply without all this exhuberance. In fact, sometimes it's even preferable. A lifetime of loving will necessitate times of sorrow along with the singing, just as Christ's love for God brought the cross along with the crown. If our life with God is based only on bubbly feelings, we're apt to fall away when the bubbles fizz out.

So joy may or may not accompany your moment of conversion, but be prepared. Joy will be part of your life with God. David rightly exclaimed, "In Thy presence is fullness of joy; in Thy right hand there are pleasures forever" (Ps. 16:11).

God's wells are full of joy; all we have to do is haul up a bucketful and drink our fill. The Ethiopian did just that when his life was invaded by the life of God.

Christ Gives True Riches

Because he had money and power, some might have dismissed this ruler as a candidate for conversion. A representative of an outreach known as Christian Women's Club once said, "Our ministry isn't to the 'down-and-outer' so much as to the 'up-and-outer.' Just because a woman has money and social status doesn't mean she doesn't need Christ. Yet these women are sometimes overlooked because we assume their well-heeled outward appearance means they have it all togther spiritually as well."

We may sometimes neglect the "up-and-outers," but God

doesn't. He seeks to draw them to Himself, just as He did the Ethiopian, so they can find the true riches only Christ can give.

CHAPTER FOUR
Nicodemus—The Religious One

A while back, I found an anonymous poem that I thought spoke profoundly to the human condition.

Oh, how I wish for that wonderful place
Called the Land of Beginning Again,
Where all our heartaches and all our mistakes
Could be dropped like a shabby old coat at the gate
And never be put on again.

Don't all of us hunger for a chance to start over, to wipe the slate clean and try again in life? Think about how many therapy centers have names like "New Beginnings" or "Creation House." Their founders understand the longing of the human soul for a chance to drop all our acquired baggage and failures and begin anew.

Jesus offered a Jewish religious leader just such an opportunity when He gave Nicodemus the chance to be born again.

Now there was a man of the Pharisees, named Nicodemus, a ruler of the Jews; this man came to Him by night, and said to Him, "Rabbi, we know that You have come from God as a teacher; for no one can do these signs that You do unless God is with him." Jesus answered and said to him, "Truly, truly, I say to you, unless one is born again, he cannot see the kingdom of God." Nicodemus said to Him, "How can a man be born when he is old? He cannot enter a second time into his mother's womb and be born, can he?" Jesus answered, "Truly, truly, I say to you, unless one is born of water and the Spirit, he cannot enter into the kingdom of God. That which is born of the flesh is flesh; and that which is born of the Spirit is spirit. Do not marvel that I said to you, 'You must be born again.' The wind blows where it wishes and you hear the sound of it, but do not know where it comes from and where it is going; so is everyone who is born of the Spirit" (John 3:1-8).

Setting the Stage

Nicodemus belonged to a religious sect known as the Pharisees, and a Pharisee's whole life was religion. When he got up in the morning, he had religion for breakfast. When he went home for lunch, he had religion. And at night he never came home and said, "Honey, what's for supper?" He knew it was going to be religion!

In the Jewish culture of Jesus' day, the Pharisees aspired to be a model of the Law lived out in daily life. Whatever the commoner did to please God, the Pharisees did and then some. If God asked them to go a mile, they tried to go two. They paid the temple tax God demanded but then went on to pay a tithe on everything they possessed as well.

Nicodemus was a ruler of these Pharisees. He was a religious professional, a preacher's preacher, so even the devout looked to him to set an example for right living. If anyone could please God, surely it was a religious person like Nicodemus.

This religious man had everything he needed to get him into heaven—if being religious could get anyone into heaven. In their meeting, however, Jesus exploded Nicodemus' source of spiritual security because the Lord refused to make religious behavior a requisite for heaven. Instead, He said, "You must be born again."

You Can Have Religion without Having God

We live in an immensely religious nation. Polls in the last few years have shown that 95 percent of us believe in God, 85 percent pray, 79 percent find strength in religion. A random survey of 3,000 households conducted by the Williamsburg Charter Foundation, found a majority of Americans favor having Congress and high school sporting events open in prayer. They approve of allowing student religious groups to hold voluntary meetings in classrooms when classes are not in session and a moment of silence in schools for voluntary prayer. A majority also favor the teaching of creationism along with evolution. And some 80 percent approve of city governments displaying a manger scene on government property ("Poll Says Religion Belongs in Public Life," *Christianity Today,* March 4, 1988, p. 38).

But multitudes of these religious people are still outside the kingdom of God. This was the condition of John Wesley, founder of Methodism, some 250 years ago.

For his first thirty-four years, Wesley was intensely religious. He was raised the son of an Anglican priest and was taught Bible reading and prayer from his strong-minded mother and an exacting headmaster. While at Oxford studying for the priesthood, he joined with others in forming a group they called the "Holy Club" to exhort each other to faithfulness in spiritual behavior. And after becoming an Anglican priest, he even went to America on a missionary venture to save the lost.

The missionary trek turned out to be a dismal failure. But as he fled America on board a ship bound for England, a man named Peter Bohler helped him realize that his lifetime of reason, ritual, and righteousness was nothing more than a barrier to saving faith. Shortly after, in a small room on a street named Aldersgate in north London, Wesley listened to someone read from Luther's *Preface to the Book of Romans.*

Wesley wrote of the experience: "About a quarter before nine, while they were describing the change that God works in the heart through faith in Christ, I felt my heart strangely warmed. I felt I did trust in Christ and Christ alone for my salvation. An assurance was given me that He had taken away my sins, even mine, and saved me from the law of sin and death." A full thirteen years earlier, Wesley had decided to live his life in service to God, but even that wasn't enough to join his life to Christ's. He needed to be born again by faith alone.

After his conversion, Wesley traveled more than 250,000 miles on horseback, preaching a thousand times a year. He wrote 400 books, established hundreds of societies, and founded schools, hospitals, and orphanages. But the difference was that this spiritual vigor wasn't generated by an attempt to gain heaven. Instead, Wesley said, it was simply a way for him to "celebrate the sovereignty of grace" (David McKenna, "That Amazing Grace," *Christianity Today,* May 13, 1988, pp. 22–23).

Wesley's experience was repeated two hundred years later by a young man named Daniel Boerman. Daniel grew up in a devoted Christian home and attended church regularly. He took the teachings he heard seriously. "Other kids criticized their parents and teachers behind their backs. Not me. Some kids swore and told dirty jokes. Not me. I was too good for that. I was a proud member of the 'Good Deeds Club,' " Daniel said.

A few years later, when he was working as a summer farm hand, a fellow worker asked, "Do you smoke?"

"No," Daniel replied.

"Do you drink?"

"No."

"Do you chase women?"

"No."

"Then," the man exclaimed in surprise, "what do you do for fun?"

The question needed no answer, because like the Pharisees, having fun wasn't a concern to Daniel. He cared only about keeping up his good behavior and good grades.

But through the sermon of a new pastor at his church, Daniel realized that he was like a man caught in quicksand who foolishly believed he could pull himself out by his own bootstraps.

Finally, he saw himself as God did. "All my good behavior and academic achievements were worthless," Daniel said.

"I felt like I was sinking in quicksand, too. [But] at last I learned to put my confidence in Christ's accomplishments instead of in my own. God's grace quietly and persistently subdued my stubborn heart" (Daniel Boerman, "A Pharisee's Confession," *Light and Life,* June 1988, pp. 20–21).

Like Nicodemus and Wesley, Boerman had to move beyond religion and upright living to come into the life of God.

Spiritual Vitality Requires a Second Birth

A great Methodist Bible teacher I studied under in the early days of my Christian pilgrimage invented his own version of

Jesus healing two blind men. Do you remember the miracles I'm referring to? When Jesus met one of the men, He simply commanded, "Receive your sight." Instantly, the man's eyes were opened. But with the other blind man, Jesus made clay out of dirt and spit and put it on the man's eyes. Then He sent the man to the Pool of Siloam to wash off the concoction. When the man obeyed, scales fell from his eyes, and he could see.

My professor theorized that the two men met by chance one day and began comparing notes on their experiences. The first said, "I used to be blind, you know, but Jesus restored my sight."

The other exclaimed, "What a coincidence! He healed me of blindness as well! Wasn't it wonderful the way He made that clay and put it on your eyes?"

The other man stared at him a moment. "You must be wrong. That isn't the way He does it, with clay on the eyes. He just says, 'Receive your sight.' I should know, because it happened to me!"

"And right then," my teacher concluded, "marked the beginning of religious denominations—the 'Mudites' and the 'Anti-Mudites.' " And I'm sure there has been mudslinging between the two ever since!

Religion focuses on differences, founded on forms and formalities, that sometimes stand in the way of faith. But the new birth has another foundation.

When Jesus talked with Nicodemus about being "born again," He didn't pull the term out of the blue. The Jewish tradition had already established the practice of calling proselytes to the Jewish faith "new born." The Greek religions used the term "born again" to describe an initiate who had a confrontation with a god. In both cases, "born again" meant the beginning of a new relationship.

Actually, there couldn't be a better analogy than birth for

what happens at conversion. The two are alike in three ways.

First, conversion marks the start of a life that's never been in existence before. Paul said it this way: "Therefore if any man is in Christ, he is a new creature; the old things passed away; behold, new things have come" (2 Cor. 5:17). When a young lady from Oklahoma ranch country was asked to read this Scripture, she drawled, "If any man be in Christ, he is a new *critter.*" But critter or creature, the punch is the same. Conversion means we've come to life spiritually.

Second, we didn't birth ourselves physically, and we can't do it spiritually, either. None of our self-effort, struggling, good behavior, or cleverness got us into the world. Our entrance was entirely a gift to us from God and our parents. So it is, Jesus said, with a birth from above. "For by grace you have been saved through faith; and that not of yourselves, it is the gift of God; not as a result of works, that no one should boast. For we are His workmanship, created in Christ Jesus" (Eph. 2:8-10).

Third, at birth we become part of a family. And just as we were born into an earthly family, we become part of a spiritual family when we're born from above.

A few years ago I was preaching at a youth camp in the Ozarks. During the week I noticed a tall, dark American Indian girl. She caught my attention first because I saw her playing basketball with the boys—and outplaying most of them. But the rest of the time, she'd usually be standing off by herself, looking like she didn't belong with anyone.

The last night of the camp, I invited those teens who wanted to give their lives to Christ to join me and the camp counselors for prayer. The Indian girl was quick to respond, and I stepped down from behind the podium to meet her. I asked why she wanted to give herself to Christ. She said, "I was an orphan. And although I was raised by a nice family, a few years ago I began to wonder about my real father. I started a search for him, but every place I looked turned out to be a dead end. I had no choice but to end my search, but the frustration I felt at not knowing my father didn't end.

"Tonight I realized that if I belong to Christ, I have a Heavenly Father, so it doesn't matter anymore who my earthly father is."

She was right. With her new birth, she became part of God's family, with a Father who will never leave her, and a multitude of brothers and sisters with whom she now belongs.

This Second Birth Is Mysterious but Real

Jesus spoke of new birth; twice Nicodemus made the same response: "How can this happen?" If Nicodemus had been around today, we'd have catagorized him "left brain dominant." He insisted there be no ambiguities. Everything had to be logical, rational, definable, concrete, and measurable if he were to consider it.

Jesus answered him with a mystery. "Look at the wind, Nicodemus. Listen to it. You don't know where it comes from or where it goes. But you feel it blowing on your face, so you know it's there. That's how it is to be born of the Spirit."

What a frustrating answer for a listener whose whole religious experience had been secured by airtight explanations! With the Spirit birth, we can't understand exactly how God does it. But it is real, nonetheless.

Think about the little caterpillar, an ugly worm crawling through life. But then he spins himself into a weblike cocoon and attaches to a twig of a tree. Hidden away in the dark, a tremendous transformation takes place. When the cocoon opens, from that gravelike wrapping emerges a magnificent butterfly. It dries its rainbow wings in the warmth of the sunlight, and instead of crawling, it opens those wings wide and begins to fly.

That's like the mystery of the new birth. God takes a worm, so insignificant, so unworthy, and puts it through the unseen and mysterious process of spiritual awakening. What emerges is a magnificent creature, totally different from what it was before. We can't explain in human terms exactly how God does it, but we know the new birth is real by the transformations it generates.

After his conversion to Christianity, a prominent United States senator was being grilled by a television talk-show host. What about empirical proof for Christianity? the interviewer insisted. What facts irrevocably validate the claims of Christ? The senator responded as he could, but finally he stopped and looked straight into the interviewer's face. "Empirical proof, historical fact—all I know is, Jesus Christ changed my life!" That fact is proof enough, but it won't be ours until we commit ourselves to trust Christ alone.

Birth Takes an Instant, but Gestation Takes Longer

Did you know that the Gospels mention Nicodemus not once but three different times? The three glimpses we're given of him may encourage you if you didn't change from worm to butterfly the very first time you heard the Gospel.

In this first encounter, Nicodemus waited until after dark to seek out Jesus. He was curious but certainly not ready to be identified with this One who claimed to be the Messiah. Jesus talked openly with the religious leader, but we have no indication that their conversation ended with Nicodemus committing himself to follow Jesus.

In John 7, the Pharisees had begun to see what a threat Christ's teachings could bring to their hold on the Jewish people, so they sent their officers to arrest Him. But the officers didn't follow through. "Why didn't you bring Jesus to us?" the Pharisees wanted to know. The officers answered, "Never did a man speak the way this man speaks" (vv. 45-46).

The Pharisees' anger boiled, and they chided the officers for their stupidity in being so taken with Jesus. To prove how ridiculous His claims were, they pointed to the fact that no Pharisee had ever believed in Him.

At this point in the debate, Nicodemus interrupted. Notice that he did *not* say, "Wait a minute. You are wrong. I'm a Pharisee, and I believe in Him!" But he also doesn't say, "You're correct in accusing Him of charlatanry. I've talked with Him personally, and I'm convinced He's deceiving all of us."

Instead, he asked a question. "Our Law does not judge a man, unless it first hears from him and knows what he is doing, does it?" (v. 51) In effect, he told the other Jewish rulers, "Why don't we listen to what He has to say before we come to any conclusions?"

Of course, these colleagues of Nicodemus had already set their minds against Jesus, and they made it clear that Nicodemus was foolish not to have done the same. "You are not also from Galilee, are you?" they sniped at him sarcastically. "Search, and see that no prophet arises out of Galilee" (v. 52).

Nicodemus made no reply to their ridicule. He seemed to be moving toward conversion, to be in spiritual gestation, but his moment of birth hadn't arrived yet.

Then, in John 19, we see Nicodemus making a clear and costly identification with Christ. After the Lord's death, Joseph of Arimathea asked Pilate for Christ's body. And John records, "And Nicodemus came also, who had first come to Him by night. . . . And so they took the body of Jesus, and bound it in linen wrappings with the spices, as is the burial custom of the Jews" (John 19:39-40).

Now, when there seemed to be nothing to gain by aligning himself with Jesus, Nicodemus identified with Him publicly. Perhaps his new birth took place quietly during the last days of

Jesus' life. Or maybe this decision to openly join himself to those who followed Jesus marked the moment of Nicodemus' conversion. The Scriptures don't tell us the exact date God recorded on Nicodemus' heavenly birth certificate. But Scripture does make clear that Nicodemus came to faith because real belief shows itself in commitment. And unveiling his allegiance to Christ at a time when His other disciples had gone into hiding showed commitment indeed.

Some people hear the Gospel once and grab right onto its truth. Others, like Nicodemus, take longer between the time the Gospel seed is planted and new life comes breaking through. Either convert is as born again as the other.

Nicodemus had to move beyond his religious practices to come to Christ, but the choice may not have been easy. It isn't an easy one for many of us. We may prefer religion to being born again for a number of reasons.

For one thing, doing good to earn God's favor keeps us solidly in control of our eternal destiny. Who needs to depend on God when righteousness by works depends only on me? No neediness or helplessness or vulnerability for us! No, sir. We are the captain of our fate, and we're not about to turn the ship over to Someone Else.

And following religion instead of receiving a new birth keeps our pride and ego alive and well. We did it our way, and we deserve the credit for our goodness.

But if, instead, we choose to be born from above, we have to abandon our pride. Eternal life is a gift of grace. We've done nothing to deserve it, done nothing at all, in fact, but chosen to receive it. God didn't give the gift because we earned it but because He loves us. That's why Jesus concluded His conversation with Nicodemus with this message: "God so loved the world, that He gave His only begotten Son, that whoever believes in Him should not perish, but have eternal life" (John 3:16). This definitive statement of conversion was first spoken not to a decadent murderer or adulterer but to a scrupuously religious man, one who already appeared to be right with God.

Are you like Nicodemus, working feverishly to earn your way into God's kingdom? Do others consider you a model of Christian living, even though you know something is missing in your life? If so, you may need to find, as did this Jewish spiritual leader, a genuine experience of the new birth.

CHAPTER FIVE
Nathanael—The Skeptic

You know people who jump on any passing bandwagon without a second thought. You'll get no questions from them about what it's going to cost, or whether it's worked for others, or how much it's going to change their lives. As long as an idea or political candidate or product or philosophy is new and comes with a halfway convincing sales pitch, they're ready to sign on the dotted line.

One critic described these "easy believers" as "so open-minded their brains are falling out." Perhaps that's too harsh, especially since those who quickly say yes often add verve and variety to an otherwise dull and routine world.

Me, I'm more of a skeptic. Maybe it's because of the tough work ethic with which I grew up, but I can't help but be a doubter, especially when it comes to get-rich-quick schemes. I know they always sound foolproof, and I know the originator always seems to have a Mercedes and a Malibu condo to prove his system works. But every time I see one of those *How to Turn a Dollar into a Million in Your Spare Time* books, I'm convinced *no one's* going to get rich except the guy who wrote the book!

Nathanael, one of Jesus' first disciples, was a skeptic. Because he was, his conversion has great encouragement to offer those of us who like to look before we leap.

> Philip found Nathanael and said to him, "We have found Him of whom Moses in the Law and also the Prophets wrote, Jesus of Nazareth, the son of Joseph." And Nathanael said to him, "Can any good thing come out of Nazareth?" Philip said to him, "Come and see." Jesus saw Nathanael coming to Him, and said of him, "Behold, an Israelite indeed, in whom is no guile!"
>
> Nathanael said to Him, "How do You know me?" Jesus answered and said to him, "Before Philip called you, when you were under the fig tree, I saw you." Nathanael answered Him, "Rabbi, You are the Son of God; You are the King of Israel." Jesus answered and said to him, "Because I said to you that I saw you under the fig tree, do you believe? You shall see greater things than these." And He said to him, "Truly, truly, I say to you, you shall see the heavens opened, and the angels of God ascending and descending upon the Son of Man" (John 1:45-51).

Setting the Stage

Philip had just met Jesus and decided he had encountered the Messiah for whom all Israel longed. Such good news couldn't be kept to himself. He must tell his friend Nathanael.

We're never told how Nathanael and Philip came to know each other. Philip was from Bethsaida, a fishing town in Galilee and also home to Peter and his brother Andrew. Andrew had believed in Jesus first and brought his brother Peter to Jesus. The next day, Jesus "found" Philip and called him to follow Him. It's not difficult to guess that Peter and Andrew might have had a hand in Jesus "finding" Philip.

Nathanael, however, was from Cana, a Galilean town much closer to Nazareth than it was to Bethsaida. But perhaps Philip and Nathanael had had business contacts. Or maybe they were related. At any rate, their friendship was such that when Philip came to faith in Jesus, he immediately wanted to bring Nathanael in on the find. If you are a businessperson, you may know what it's like to come on a great stock, one that's selling low and is headed sky-high. You buy it, of course, but you're barely off the phone to your broker before you're dialing again, this time to your friend so he can cash in on the great news too. Such is the pattern of those, like Philip, who find Christ and then can't wait to share Him with someone else.

Nathanael Considered Jesus

In the exhuberance of his newfound faith, Philip exclaimed to Nathanael, "We have found Him of whom Moses in the Law and also the Prophets wrote, Jesus of Nazareth, the son of Joseph!"

Nathanael could have responded to this declaration a number of ways. He might have *agreed instantly*. "You've found the Messiah! That's incredible, Philip! Take me to Him, so I can follow Him too."

Nathanael could also have *disagreed instantly*. "Come on, Philip. Our people have been waiting a thousand years for the Messiah, and now you say He's all of a sudden arrived? And He's from a family no one's ever heard of? And He's chosen to reveal Himself to *you*, even before He presents Himself to the Pharisees in Jerusalem? Really, Philip. Listen to yourself! Surely when God sends the Messiah, it'll be to a center of power, not to a village in Galilee. And we won't hear the news of his arrival from your fishing buddies. Fake messiahs are a dime a dozen. Let the Sanhedrin give your teacher their seal of approval, then talk to me again, all right?"

Many of us aren't quick to respond to new ideas. You'll hear us say things like: "The best ways are the old ways"; "We've never done it like that before"; "That isn't how I was raised"; "If that plan is so good, someone would have thought of it before this."

Do you cheer for the Brooklyn Dodgers, request penny postcards from the mail service, and tell a kid with a floppy disk to see a chiropractor? If you do, you may be a person who automatically rejects new ideas just because they're unfamiliar.

Not Nathanael. When Philip talked about the Messiah, Nathanael didn't reject his idea, even though listening to it might demand radical changes in his life.

Nathanael did consider what Philip had to say. No easy yes, no instant no, but rather a highly skeptical "maybe, but. . . ."

Are you a skeptic? If you are, the *Random House Dictionary* defines you as "a person who frequently questions ideas or facts widely accepted." A skeptic isn't the same as a doubter. A doubter has the facts he needs to make a decision but chooses instead to respond in suspicion and distrust to avoid having to commit himself. But a skeptic deliberates because he's seeking all the facts before he decides. He looks before he leaps because he intends to swim in the pond into which he's jumping.

Jesus had harsh words for doubters, but of skeptics He spoke kindly. He called Nathanael "an Israelite indeed in whom there is no guile." He wasn't accusing Nathanael of being naive. He meant instead that Nathanael didn't cling to a hidden agenda. His questions weren't meant to manipulate or maneuver or make his way around responsibility. With Nathanael, what you see is what you get. His skepticism marked an honest seeker, and Christ responded positively to him.

When Jesus told His Parable of the Sower, He said that some seed doesn't bear fruit because it falls on shallow soil, grows up quickly, but soon withers in the heat of the day. Doesn't this sound like our first-on-the-bandwagon friend who grabs onto any new idea but just as quickly abandons it for another? We can't expect a genuine conversion from him.

But Jesus also said that some seed doesn't grow because it doesn't even have a chance to take root when it falls on the rock-hard earth beside the road. And those of us who won't even consider new ideas provide just such unfriendly soil for God's Word to grow in us.

God's Word bears fruit, Jesus said, when it falls on the good soil. Often it's the skeptics, like Nathanael, who become good soil for God's Word because they hear the Word and then *consider it.* They poke and probe. They question and query. They watch and weigh. To Philip's announcement that he'd found the Messiah, Nathanael responded with a question. "Can anything good come out of Nazareth?"

A conversation with a friend stimulated Nathanael to consider Christ. That's the way it happens for many of us. Sometimes a *crisis* can cause us to consider Christ. A close brush with death or the loss of a loved one can alert us to spiritual questions. But God doesn't always use a catastrophe to pique our interest in His claims; sometimes "the kindness of God leads you to repentance" (Rom. 2:4).

Abdul was a devout Muslim when he came to America to finish his college education. His schoolwork was slowed, however, by recurring back problems for which he was to have an operation. The thought of the surgery terrified Abdul, and he admitted his terror to a friend during lunch the day before his final presurgery checkup.

Two ladies at the next table approached Abdul. "We hope you'll forgive us for overhearing," one apologized, "but we couldn't help but hear how concerned you are about having surgery. We are Christians, and we wondered if we might have your permission to pray for you." At this point, Abdul had no interest in the Christian faith, but the ladies' concern touched him, and he agreed to let them pray.

The next day, when he saw his doctor, he was greeted with some surprising news. "Sir," the doctor told him, "we think we have a problem with your CAT scan. The one you took this morning indicates there's nothing wrong with your back. Of course we know that's not the case, so we must have mixed up your records. Would you mind having a second scan done?" Abdul agreed, and a second test was taken. But this time both the doctor and his patient were in for a surprise. The second scan matched the first. The problems with Abdul's back had disappeared; no surgery was warranted.

Abdul was so amazed by what had transpired that he left the office and headed straight for a nearby church. "Is there someone here who could tell me about Christ?" he asked the startled church secretary. God's unmerited goodness to this Muslim man caused him to consider Jesus, and that day he gladly gave his heart to the Lord.

God can use a number of instigators to move us to consider receiving what He offers. What's important is that we do stop and consider, not jumping too quickly, but not shutting Him out either.

Nathanael Wrestled with Confusion

Sometimes people are skeptical because they feel they're being asked to assemble a puzzle with pieces that simply don't fit. Nathanael may have felt this way.

Nathanael knew the Old Testament teachings about the Messiah. He likely could have told us that:

● Genesis 18:18 says the Messiah would be the promised seed of Abraham.

● Isaiah 9:7 says the Prophet would be heir to the throne of David.

• Micah 5:2 teaches that the Messiah would be born in Bethlehem of Judea.

• Isaiah 7:14 says His mother would be a virgin.

• Zechariah 9:9 describes the triumphal entry into the city of Jerusalem on the foal of a donkey.

• Zechariah 11:12 describes the betrayal of the Messiah for thirty pieces of silver.

Not one of the prophesies made any mention at all of Nazareth, and this alleged Messiah that Philip presented hailed from Nazareth. Nazareth? The fact confused Nathanael because it didn't seem logical that the Messiah would come from this place. Nazareth didn't fit with Nathanael's understanding of God and how He worked.

When spiritual truth confuses us, we can be tempted to reject it. But Nathanael didn't do that. When his friend Philip invited him to look for answers to his confusion, he accepted the challenge. "Come and see," Philip said, and Nathanael did.

Nathanael would have felt very comfortable with the people in Berea to whom Paul would bring the Gospel several years later. The book of Acts says, "Now [the Bereans] were more noble-minded than those in Thessalonica, for they received the word with great eagerness, examining the Scriptures daily, to see whether these things were so" (Acts 17:11).

The skeptical mind can examine the Christian faith. You don't have to hang your brain in the vestibule when you come to church. It's not out of line to ask questions. Jesus not only wants your heart; He wants your head. Love the Lord with all your *mind*, soul, body, and strength, Scripture admonishes us. If you're selling used cars and you know your autos run, you won't flinch when a customer comes in with his mechanic in tow. In fact, you'll encourage him to have your cars checked out. Authenticity invites investigation. Christ can boldly allow our scrutiny because He knows He is what He claims to be and can do what He says He will. If we genuinely seek Him, we're going to find He's for real.

Back in the early 1900s, the atheistic movement of Great Britain hired two of the most brilliant attorneys of the day, Gilbert West and Lord Littleton, to disprove Christianity. West's assigned task was to disprove the conversion of Saul, and Littleton was charged to discredit the resurrection of Christ.

The two men worked independently, but when they finally met, each prefaced his introduction with a profuse apology to the other. It seemed that in the course of the men's exploration of the Scriptures, both had become converts to Christianity! (George W. Truett, *A Quest for Souls*, Harper and Brothers)

Sir William Ramey, an archeologist and professor at Oxford, set out for Israel on an archeological expedition to prove the Book of Acts was historically inaccurate. After a short time there, he wrote to his atheistic parents, "This is going to be a little more difficult than I thought." Five years later, he wrote, "There is much data showing strong evidence in favor of the historicity of the Book of Acts." Three years after that, he said, "You never put a spade in the ground, but it reveals the Book of Acts to be true. I have become a Christian!" And five years later, he wrote a book documenting the truth of the Bible from an archeological perspective.

Even the author of the famous novel *Ben Hur*, General Lew Wallace, began his exploration of Scripture in an attempt to prove that Jesus Christ was not who He claimed to be, and wound up acknowledging Christ as his Lord (George W. Truett, *A Quest for Souls*, Harper and Brothers).

To those skeptical of Christianity, I like to say, "Don't knock it until you've tried it." Nathanael didn't let his confusion harden into spiritual coldness. He let it spur him to seek Christ.

Nathanael Confronted Jesus

When Jesus saw Nathanael coming toward Him, He said, "Behold, an Israelite indeed, in whom is no guile."

Nathanael didn't say, "Thank you for such kind words." Once again he showed that his natural skepticism was firmly in place. "How did you know me?" he asked the Lord.

"Before Philip called you, when you were under the fig tree, I saw you."

In a quiet display of omniscience, Jesus allowed Nathanael to see His God-power unveiled. This skeptic came seeking, and Christ responded to his quest. Now it was Nathanael's turn to respond to the evidence before him, and he chose to believe Christ's claim to be the Messiah. Jesus accepted him gladly and graciously.

When we come to Christ, He does what we expect and then much, much more. He assured Nathanael, "Because I said to you that I saw you under the fig tree, do you believe? You shall see greater things than these! . . . You shall see the heavens opened, and the angels of God ascending and descending upon the Son of Man." It was as if Christ were saying, "Nathanael, you haven't seen anything yet!" And to be sure, Nathanael hadn't. In the very next chapter of John, Jesus attended a wedding in Nathanael's hometown of Cana and miraculously changed plain water into the best wine. From there He went on to heal the sick and calm the seas and raise the dead. And He Himself exploded from the grave just three years later. Truly, Nathanael had no idea of the magnificent miracles he would witness.

The Apostle Paul puts it this way: "Eye hath not seen, nor ear heard, neither have entered into the heart of man, the things which God hath prepared for them that love Him" (1 Cor. 2:9, KJV). When we confront Christ, He'll respond to us.

Nathanael Confessed Christ

Nathanael said to Jesus, "Rabbi, You are the Son of God; You are the King of Israel."

Nathanael knew the Scriptures well enough to know exactly what he was saying as he spoke these words. No Jew ever lightly called another "the Son of God," or "the King of Israel." When the Pharisees heard Jesus calling Himself the Son of God, they tried to have him put to death for blasphemy. To apply these names to anyone had serious consequences. At the moment of Nathanael's confession, he was converted. But it wasn't saying these words that brought him into God's kingdom; it was the faith that these words expressed.

I sometimes meet people who tell me they've prayed a prayer inviting Jesus into their lives, but nothing happened when they did. Therefore they think the Gospel is little more than a superstitious hoax. But I disagree. If they called Christ "Lord" and nothing changed in their lives, then they're telling me their prayer wasn't accompanied by faith. Either they didn't believe the Gospel's truth, or they didn't understand it adequately enough to come to faith.

But Nathanael's words of faith sprang from a heart of faith. He saw the evidence and chose to believe it. He would follow Jesus, trusting Him to be the promised Messiah and Saviour of the world.

With this confession, the skeptic became a believer. He didn't dive into the kingdom, but slowly and pensively he came, asking questions, mulling over the answers. And Christ welcomed him, for once this skeptic believed, he made an excellent disciple! Nathanael followed Christ faithfully, through both the success of His ministry and the apparent defeat of the cross, and then stayed on to be part of establishing a church that turned the world upside down. Do you know a skeptic? Don't let his cynicism keep you from sharing Christ's love and the Gospel story. Just as it was for Nathanael, conversion may be just ahead for your skeptical friend.

CHAPTER SIX
Woman at the Well—The Resistant One

Some of Jesus' encounters with people make for great drama. Nicodemus sought Christ in the dark of night. Another time, a demon-possessed boy threw himself, writhing and screaming, at Jesus' feet.

In contrast, His meeting with a woman at a Samaritan well seems decidedly commonplace. Thirsty traveler meets local citizen with waterpot and asks for help. Nothing seemingly spiritual or supernatural or mystical here. Yet we'll see as the story unfolds that this ordinary encounter would change the woman's life and the lives of many in her town for eternity.

How many dozens of encounters do we experience like this every day as we go about our business? Think of the cashier at the convenience store where you regularly stop for coffee, or the fellow parent you end up sitting next to at your children's swim meet, or the sales rep you deal with occasionally at work. We never know when God has been at work, engineering one of these "chance" encounters for His purposes, either to minister to us or to minister through us to another.

He [Jesus] left Judea, and departed again into Galilee. And He had to pass through Samaria. So He came to a city of Samaria, called Sychar, near the parcel of ground that Jacob gave to his son Joseph; and Jacob's well was there. Jesus therefore, being wearied from His journey, was sitting thus by the well. It was about the sixth hour. There came a woman of Samaria to draw water. Jesus said to her, "Give Me a drink." For His disciples had gone away into the city to buy food (John 4:3-8).

Setting the Stage

The Lord and His disciples were walking north from Judea back to their home in Galilee, following the shortest route through Samaria. Now it was noon and the travelers were tired and hungry. The disciples went on into a nearby city to pick up lunch, but Jesus, "weary from the journey," stayed behind. He sat down by Jacob's well to rest, and when a woman approached, the thirsty Teacher asked her for a much-needed drink of water.

On that day, God used this meeting at a well in Samaria to quench a woman's thirst for satisfaction. But the woman wasn't a ready recipient of the living water Christ offered. During their interaction, she threw up eight barriers between herself and God. Those barriers are the same ones people struggle with today as they reach for heaven.

Jesus Overcame the Barrier of Prejudice

The Samaritan woman therefore said to Him, "How is it that You, being a Jew, ask me for a drink since I am a Samaritan woman?" (For Jews have no dealings with Samaritans) (John 4:9).

When Jesus asked the woman for a drink, she replied, "I'm

a Samaritan, and you Jews think you are better than we are."
She may have reveled in the chance to have the upper hand
with a hated Jew. She had something He needed, so this could
be her moment to make Him squirm a little.

This prejudice between the Jews and the Samaritans had
deep roots, going back as far as 720 B.C. Some of the Jews in
the central and northern parts of Palestine intermarried with
the Gentile Assyrians who invaded their land. Because of their
roots, the people of Samaria were considered half-breeds and
compromisers by their brothers in southern Palestine who had
stayed pure.

But the rift became even more complicated 300 years later
when Ezra and Nehemiah began rebuilding the holy temple
which had been destroyed by the Assyrians. Samaritans offered to help with the work, but their offer was refused. So a
renegade Jew named Manasses, married to a Samaritan, retali-
ated by building a rival temple on top of Mount Gerizim (located in view of the well where Jesus met the Samaritan woman).

Because of these clashes, Samaritans hated Jews. Later in
His ministry, Jesus sent messengers into Samaria to arrange
lodging for His party as He traveled to Jerusalem, but the
Samaritans refused to house Him because He was headed for
the Jews' holy city (Luke 9:52-53). Their hostility so incensed
James and John that they asked permission to call down fire
from heaven and consume the inhospitable Samaritans. Prejudice flows both ways.

But Jesus stood against this evil cancer of prejudice. In a
parable He told later, Jesus chose as His "hero" a good
Samaritan.

Though Jesus has little tolerance for prejudice, we can let it
keep us from His kingdom. One minister said, "When God
called me to commitment, He spoke through a woman preacher in a denomination I had little use for. That night my prejudice kept me from responding to the invitation she extended to

follow the Lord, even though I knew God was speaking to me. Though the Lord graciously gave me another chance, my prejudice almost kept me from finding my place of service in God's work."

Is prejudice keeping you from hearing God's call? Do you refuse to listen because God chooses to speak through those who don't dress as well as you or aren't as sophisticated as you or come from a racial or ethnic heritage you feel isn't as good as yours? The Samaritan woman probably felt justified in her hatred of the Jews. After all, the Jews treated Samaritans with disdain. When the Pharisees wanted to slander Jesus, they said, "You are a Samaritan and have a demon" (John 8:48). Apparently in their minds, one malady was as bad as the other. But Jesus assaulted the barrier of prejudice by ignoring it. Instead of trying to reconcile their racial and religious differences, He simply went on to turn the woman toward the living water He could supply.

It's interesting to note later in the story that when this woman believed in Christ, the Lord and His disciples stayed in her town several days, helping many Samaritans come to faith. Jews risking defilement by staying with unholy Samaritan half-breeds? Never! Samaritans listening to religious truth taught to them by a Jew? Impossible! Yet it happened. Faith in Christ broke through the barrier of prejudice.

He Confronted the Barrier of Ignorance

> Jesus answered and said to her, "If you knew the gift of God, and who it is who says to you, 'Give Me a drink,' you would have asked Him, and He would have given you living water" (John 4:10).

Jesus told the woman there was truth she simply didn't know. In a 1988 best-selling book called *The Closing of the*

American Mind, University of Chicago philosophy professor Allen Bloom eloquently decries our society's turning away from absolutes. We're a nation of moral illiterates when it comes to knowing the simple truths of God's plan for mankind. Some think Christmas means little more than the birth of goodwill, incarnated in Santa Claus. We're led to believe that Easter celebrates the return of spring, delivered in the kindly Easter Bunny's basket. Many in our world haven't had an opportunity to reject the Gospel because they don't even know what it is.

How different this is from American generations before us. One family I know visited a historical village in the Midwest at Christmastime. All through the village, reenactments of Christmas celebrations of 100 years ago went on. The family decided their children would enjoy seeing an elementary school Christmas program as it would have been presented a century ago, so the foursome crowded into the one-room school building dimly lit by kerosene lamps and heated only by a potbellied, wood-burning stove. Little girls in braids and calico dresses and boys relying on suspenders to keep their trousers up sang carols and gave recitations. But to the parents, the biggest surprise of the day came when they heard the topics of those recitations.

There was no general feel-good mush about jolly old Saint Nick and humankind's need for the spirit of love. "The children spoke clearly of Christ being sent from God to take away our sins. Some of their poems even ended in a challenge to admit our need of His forgiveness and give our hearts to Him," the mother said. "I knew this historical village had no religious affiliation; these children were simply presenting what were commonly known truths to generations before us."

But times have changed, and in America at the close of the twentieth century, many people are ignorant of who Christ is and what He came to do, just as the Samaritan woman was.

But Jesus didn't turn from her when He saw the barrier of her ignorance. Instead, He went on to instruct her in the truth.

He Met the Barrier of Misunderstanding

> She said to Him, "Sir, You have nothing to draw with and the well is deep; where then do You get that living water?" (John 4:11)

When Jesus spoke of living water, the woman misunderstood. She was trying to understand spiritual truth in human terms. It's the same mistake Nicodemus made when Jesus told him of his need to be born again. Nicodemus heard only a physical experience in Jesus' words and couldn't grasp the spiritual truth the Lord was trying to picture for him.

How easy this is to do! It's particularly easy to misunderstand in issues of spiritual truth because many of God's ways of working seem so illogical to our way of thinking: It's better to give than receive. . . . You can win by losing. You can find life by giving up your life. How many of these truths make rational sense in our high-tech, win-by-intimidation and go-for-the-gusto world? And to make matters worse, many of God's truths don't just seem mysterious; they actually are mysterious. We can't bottle them, color-code them, and analyze them statistically. We can't identify their basic components and conjure them up in a laboratory on demand.

Faith, godliness, eternal life, God's kingdom—Scripture describes all of them as mysteries. As Agatha Christie fans will tell you, unraveling mysteries takes time and attention and investigation. And the solving of mysteries leaves plenty of room for misunderstanding along the way.

The Samaritan woman's misunderstanding of Jesus' mysterious words became a barrier to her faith, but even this barrier was battered down.

He Recognized the Barrier of Unbelief

"You are not greater than our father Jacob, are You,
who gave us the well, and drank of it himself, and his
sons, and his cattle?" (John 4:12)

This time, the woman wasn't misunderstanding Jesus. She
simply didn't believe what He was saying. "Who do You think
You are?" she was asking Him. "Do You think You are greater
than our ancestor who gave us this well?" She understood
what the Lord had said very plainly. Indeed, He fully intended
to set Himself above Jacob because that higher position rightly
belonged to Him. The woman understood clearly, but she
didn't believe His claim.

I believe the one sin God will not forgive is this sin of
unbelief. Is my stand too strong? I don't think so. What is it
that sends people to hell? Is it the sin of stealing or murder or
lying? We tend to busy ourselves setting up a scale of mea-
surement, comparing the badness of one sin against another,
in an attempt to determine which is worst of all. When we do,
I think we're missing the mark.

Religious groups often play havoc with Christ's teaching on
what we call the "unpardonable sin." One woman was told
she'd committed it when she divorced her alcoholic husband.
Actually, the man had already abandoned her, after brutally
abusing both her and their three children, so the divorce was
more of a formality than anything. A well-meaning but sorely
misinformed man in her church made it clear that in her action,
she'd committed the unpardonable sin.

In another tragic misunderstanding of the meaning of the
unpardonable sin, one former Christian leader referred to it as
a major factor in his decision to abandon his wife of forty years
and move in with a woman twenty years his junior. "I struggled with the decision to leave my wife," he said, "until I

realized there was only one unpardonable sin: blaspheming the Holy Spirit. Therefore, even if what I was choosing to do was sinful, God had to forgive me because what I was doing wasn't unpardonable."

What confusion! An important Scriptural teaching has been used for such ridiculous purposes, because we're not clear on what the Lord means when He talks about the unpardonable sin.

Jesus said, "Any sin and blasphemy shall be forgiven men, but blasphemy against the Spirit shall not be forgiven" (Matt. 12:31). But what does it mean to blaspheme the Holy Spirit? I believe it means the continual rejection of the Holy Spirit as He tries to reveal Christ as Saviour to us. It's not so much a one-time act as it is an attitude which continually says no to the Spirit's wooing. That's why it's so important to respond to the Lord when we sense Him calling us to Himself.

He Cleared the Barrier of Confusion

> The woman said to Him, "Sir, give me this water, so I will not be thirsty, nor come all the way here to draw" (John 4:15).

She was confused. She thought Jesus was promising to supply her with physical water for as long as she lived. Who would pass up an offer as good as that? No more trudging to the well in the heat of the day. No more headaches from the weight of the waterpot on her head. She saw commitment to Christ as a kind of heavenly lottery ticket which could be exchanged for a life of ease when she cashed it in.

Others who heard Jesus preach shared her confusion. When He called Himself the Bread of Life, many of His hearers expected Him to reward their devotion with a lifetime supply of free baked goods. When He spoke of a kingdom that wouldn't end, some of His followers quarreled about their royal positions. He promised riches to the poor, and some of them began planning country estates and slaves of their own.

This same confusion about Christ's promise of abundant life exists today. If I follow Him, what does He guarantee? If I follow His will in my choice of professions, can I expect success, promotions, and respect? If I take the spouse of His choosing, am I guaranteed she'll never leave me, and we'll sail through life in unmarred wedded bliss? Is He guaranteeing I'll have no problems with my children, no struggles with my health, no disruptions in my relationships? Some seem to think so.

Like the woman at the well, we may be confused about His claims. We think He promises peace *instead of* pain, but instead He offers peace *in the midst of* pain. His power doesn't mean we'll be able to run from all sadness; instead He assures us He'll be *with us* through sadness, and that in His power, He'll turn the sadness for our good. Dr. J. Sidlow Baxter, noted preacher and author, defined peace for me this way: "Peace," he said, "is not the absence of pain; it is the presence of God."

All we have to do is look at the Teacher's life and realize we need to take a closer look at His message. If His promises of riches meant material wealth, then why did He not even have a place to lay His head? If His promises of power meant earthly rule, why did He slip away when they tried to make Him king?

Don't misunderstand. Committing our lives to Christ may result in material good. Because of His presence in our home, I've experienced a more deeply satisfying marriage than I could have created on my own. The work He's chosen for me fulfills me spiritually, yes, but also intellectually and creatively. And following His principles for living, I'm healthier and financially more solid than I ever could have been without His direction.

But these benefits are secondary to His most important gifts. I've known the incredible stability His peace can bring in times of trouble. And when I've been lonely, He's given me His love and companionship. In times of discouragement, He has restored my soul, just as He promised He would. These gifts far surpass any material reality.

But the Samaritan woman couldn't see beyond the material to the spiritual reality Christ was offering, so her confusion built a barrier to faith.

He Came against the Barrier of Sin

He said to her, "Go, call your husband, and come here." The woman answered and said, "I have no husband." Jesus said to her, "You have well said, 'I have no husband'; for you have had five husbands, and the one whom you now have is not your husband; this you have said truly" (John 4:16-18).

From His behavior, we can see Jesus had no degree from a school of psychology that taught indirect counseling. He didn't wait for her to decide that her behavior was wrong; instead, He directly confronted the woman with her sin.

He didn't try to justify her wrongdoing. He could have said, "You're living in immorality, but don't feel bad because everybody's doing it, and I know how hurt you were in your last divorce, and your self-concept is terribly low."

He also didn't overlook her sin by balancing it against her better attributes. He didn't say, "My, what a lovely waterpot you have. And you carry it so gracefully too."

Her sin stood in the way of her conversion, and Christ was determined to break through this barrier.

Before conversion can occur, we have to own up to our sins. God doesn't require this because He wants to degrade us or humiliate us. We don't admit our sinfulness for His sake but for ours. Those who are well don't seek out a doctor. Those who are clean won't ask to be washed. Likewise, we won't understand our need for a Saviour until we are sure we can't save ourselves. Claiming our sin makes us needy, and once we're needy, Christ stands ready and eager to rescue us from our need. He doesn't ask us to confess our sins so we can clean up our lives; He wants us to own our wrongs so He can deliver us from them.

He Resolved the Barrier of Guilt

> The woman said to Him, "Sir, I perceive that You are
> a prophet" (John 4:19).

To this woman's credit, she didn't try to blame someone else for her sin. She didn't talk about her parents' wrongdoings or her husbands' problems or her boyfriend's sin. Isn't that often a temptation? God points to evil in our lives, and we respond with, "Yes, but the other person said. . . ." Maybe we do this instinctively because the habit begins so early. Kids can adeptly pass the blame before they are old enough to pass the applesauce at dinner. "He made me do it!" "She hit me first."

But even children come by this tendency legitimately. When God called Adam to task for the very first sin, what was Adam's split-second response? "The woman whom Thou gavest to be with me, she gave me from the tree, and I ate" (Gen. 3:12). First Adam blames Eve, then he even blames God for his sin.

The Samaritan woman tried a different, and perhaps more adult, technique for covering the guilt she felt. She turned the spotlight away from herself and onto Jesus, hoping that her bit of flattery might make Him forget His accusation. After Adam and Eve's sin, they hid themselves from the Lord, just as the Samaritan woman tried to cover her guilt by hiding behind these kind words. Maybe Jesus would feel good about what she said and forget about her sin.

But Christ had no intention of leaving her wallowing in the bog of her guilt. He didn't reveal her sin just to make her squirm; He revealed it so He could excise it, if only the woman would allow Him to.

He Sidestepped the Barrier of Religion

"Our fathers worshiped in this mountain, and you people say that in Jerusalem is the place where men ought to worship." Jesus said to her, "Woman, believe Me, an hour is coming when neither in this mountain, nor in Jerusalem, shall you worship the Father. You worship that which you do not know; we worship that which we know, for salvation is from the Jews. But an hour is coming, and now is, when the true worshipers shall worship the Father in spirit and truth" (John 4:20-23).

Even 2,000 years ago, the enemy was using religion as a weapon to keep a seeker from conversion. It's a technique he's used thousands of times since.

The Samaritan woman used religion to shield herself from Christ. She tried to lure Him into the theological debate of the day concerning where worship should take place. (If she lived in our century, would she bring up televangelists or the African famine? It's quite likely.)

Dr. Frank Barker, a renowned Presbyterian pastor, says of her action:

Jesus probably smiled to Himself when He heard her question. She was to be the first of many who would

try this ploy when they realized receiving His life
might cost them something. Belief in the Gospel ne-
cessitates a willingness to change our lives. When we
receive Christ, we embrace a Saviour, but we also
bow before the Lord. Even today, those who want no-
fault salvation quickly hide behind intellectual difficul-
ties to keep them from revealing their own need.
Sometimes the plea of "I don't understand" actually
means "I don't want to change."

Dr. Barker tells of a two-hour exchange with a man who
was supposedly riddled with intellectual reservations about the
Christian faith. The man jumped from one question to another,
and though Dr. Barker and another Christian tried to answer,
the "seeker" seemed to move no closer toward a commitment
to Christ.

"Later," Dr. Barker said, "I found out the man was living in
adultery and also had a reputation for highly questionable business practices. I wondered then if his reluctances about the
Gospel were actually intellectual or moral ones instead. Perhaps his questions served to justify keeping God at arm's
length, so nothing in his life would have to change" (Frank
Barker with Maureen Rank, *Encounters with Jesus*, Victor
Books, p. 13).

Jesus knew the Samaritan woman's real need, so instead of
giving way to wrangling over religious rites, He gently drew
her back to her own sin and His solution.

The Barriers Crumbled

The woman said to Him, "I know that Messiah is coming (He who is called Christ); when that One comes,
He will declare all things to us." Jesus said to her, "I
who speak to you am He" (John 4:25-26).

This was the message Jesus had tried to convey to the woman when He first promised her living water, but too many barriers stood in the way. She couldn't hear or believe the truth He offered. But He patiently confronted each barrier and surmounted it, so now she could not only understand the truth but also respond to Him in faith. She turned and ran back to the village, calling to all she knew, "Come, see a man who told me all the things that I have done; this is not the Christ, is it?" (John 4:29) Her words must have had impact, because people came, and Scripture says, "From that city many of the Samaritans believed in Him because of the word of the woman" (John 4:39). These who came then confronted Christ for themselves and told her, "It is no longer because of what you said that we believe, for we have heard for ourselves and know that this One is indeed the Savior of the world" (John 4:42).

The Samaritan woman didn't have to break down her friends' barriers to belief. Jesus would handle that task, just as He had with her. All she needed to do was invite them to listen to Him. They soon discovered that getting close to Jesus can be dangerous because He's catching! He can obliterate all obstacles and bring those He chooses to new life in Him.

Have you erected a barrier between you and Christ? Is a wall standing between you and conversion? Let Christ assault it. He can help you come to the conversion you long to experience.

CHAPTER SEVEN
Paul—The God-Hater

Every so often, certain people undergo a transformation which is so striking that they become the symbol for an entire age or a movement or a belief system.

It's impossible to talk very long about true love without bringing up the story of Romeo and Juliet or the Duke of Windsor, who gave up the throne of England for the woman he adored.

Proponents of passive resistance can barely complete a speech without a reference to India's Ghandi or Martin Luther King and his "I have a dream" challenge. Rock and roll means Elvis Presley and the Beatles; baseball legends begin with Babe Ruth.

The conversion of the Apostle Paul is one such "hinge" story for Christianity. The effect of his conversion permeated the growth of the early church. His story is as central to the New Testament as Abraham's was to the Old Testament. The actual incident of his encounter with the Lord is recorded three different times in the Book of Acts, and parts of it are chronicled in another four places in the epistles. No other conversion story matches it!

The importance the Holy Spirit has chosen to give to this particular conversion should make us sit up and take notice. Paul's experience has important things to teach us about what can happen when we meet the risen Lord.

> Now Saul, still breathing threats and murder against the disciples of the Lord, went to the high priest, and asked for letters from him to the synagogues at Damascus, so that if he found any belonging to the Way, both men and women, he might bring them bound to Jerusalem. And it came about that as he journeyed, he was approaching Damascus, and suddenly a light from heaven flashed around him; and he fell to the ground, and heard a voice saying to him, "Saul, Saul, why are you persecuting Me?" And he said, "Who art Thou, Lord?" And He said, "I am Jesus whom you are persecuting, but rise, and enter the city, and it shall be told you what you must do." And the men who traveled with him stood speechless, hearing the voice, but seeing no one. And Saul got up from the ground, and though his eyes were open, he could see nothing; and leading him by the hand, they brought him into Damascus. . . .
>
> Now for several days he was with the disciples who were at Damascus, and immediately he began to proclaim Jesus in the synagogues, saying, "He is the Son of God." And all those hearing him continued to be amazed, and were saying, "Is this not he who in Jerusalem destroyed those who called on this name, and who had come here for the purpose of bringing them bound before the chief priests?" But Saul kept increasing in strength and confounding the Jews who lived at Damascus by proving that this Jesus is the Christ (Acts 9:1-8, 19-22).

Setting the Stage

What an unusual history Paul had! One scholar says, "Three elements of the world's life of that day—Greek culture, Roman citizenship, and Hebrew religion—met in the apostle to the Gentiles" (*The New Compact Bible Dictionary*, T. Alton Bryant, editor, Zondervan, p. 436).

Paul was born in Tarsus, a Greco-Roman city on the Mediterranean Sea, so he grew up comfortable with Greek culture and proud of the advantages his Roman citizenship provided. Yet Paul was born of purest Jewish blood, the son of a Pharisee, and raised in strict Jewish orthodoxy. "A Hebrew of Hebrews," he rightly called himself (Phil.3:5). At perhaps age thirteen, he was sent to Jerusalem to study under Gamaliel, the respected Pharisee and teacher of the Law.

Paul first appears in Scripture as Saul, the one who held the coats of those stoning Stephen to death. "Saul was in hearty agreement with putting him to death," the writer of Acts records. Some devout men came to bury Stephen, but even as they did, "Saul began ravaging the church, entering house after house; and dragging off men and women, he would put them in prison" (Acts 8:1, 3). And just going after those in Jerusalem wasn't enough for Saul; he asked permission from the Jewish rulers to chase believers who had fled to Damascus.

It was on his way to Damascus that he was felled by a blinding light and encountered the Lord. In Saul's conversion, three elements are unique, but three elements are common to us all.

Paul Was an Unusual Candidate

If you're about to start a mail-order business, you'll only succeed if you approach people who want what you are selling. A candymaker, for example, wouldn't want to distribute his catalog of chocolates and peanut brittle to a mailing list of dieters. That's why you can rent lists of gamblers, Rolls Royce owners, wealthy persons, gourmet cooks, motorcycle enthusiasts, persons who raise tropical fish, antinuclear activists, and many more. And these prospect lists get more specific all the time. If you believe your product will sell best to women who are under the age of sixty, who are in the $25,000-and-over income category, who live in cold climates, and who enjoy hiking, you could rent a list of just such people.

But if the first-century church had looked for a list of those likely to be warm to Christianity, I know one name *guaranteed* not to be on it: Saul of Tarsus. Saul not only wasn't interested in Christianity; he vehemently hated the disciples and thought God did too. Nothing pleased him more than seeing them put to death. His behavior demonstrates the kind of "righteous" mean streak we see today in some terrorists who believe they're doing heaven a great favor by ridding earth of those they consider unworthy.

It's one thing to try to share your faith with someone who's uninformed about Christianity; it's quite another to approach someone who feels a holy calling to vehemently oppose everything you believe. Paul was as open to becoming a Christian as Phyllis Schlafly would be to initiating a Revive-the-Equal-Rights-Amendment movement.

Most converts to Christianity don't start out as enemies of the Cross. And most enemies of the Cross don't become converted. So in this sense Paul's conversion was unusual, though he emphatically proves that it can happen even to the least likely prospect.

Back during the campus unrest of the seventies, I was holding meetings during Religious Emphasis Week at a college in Kansas City. During that week, a girl named Linda gave her heart to Christ. It wasn't until later I understood how remarkable this conversion really was.

Linda was the campus religion-hater. At a mention of the Gospel, she'd let loose an explosion of profanity. So great was her hostility toward spiritual things that she'd ferret out campus prayer meetings so she could hassle and harangue the participants into quitting. No one dreamed she'd be a candidate for conversion.

But on Thursday night of our week of meetings, she learned there was to be a rap session in one of the dorms at 10:00. Seeing another opportunity to bedevil the efforts of the religious freaks, she headed for the meeting. But just as she entered the meeting room, she heard her name. One of the students was praying for her! And at that moment, God broke through the mile-high wall she'd erected around her heart and claimed her as His own. Linda not only gave her heart to Christ but insisted on making a public admission of her changed life before the entire student body.

The Sauls and the Lindas may be unusual in the community of faith, but they do exist. When you see people like Saul, do you pray for their conversion? What about the newspaper editor who consistently attacks Christian causes? Or the manager of the video rental store who fills his shelves with filthy movies? Or those heading the groups who promote killing unborn babies? Or the rock stars whose lives typify the worst in decadent living? Do we believe Christ could reach these?

I'm always challenged when I hear of the conversion of someone like Madelyn Murray O'Hare's son. Though his mother's name is synonymous with antichristian activism, this young man found Christ. But if I had known him before his conversion, would I have written him off as the enemy or seen him as one in need of Christ?

The believers may have thought Saul a hopeless case, but God didn't. And after his conversion, Saul (who was later called Paul) gathered all the passion he'd poured out fighting

God and turned it to energize the preaching of the Gospel. We often think people have to be infected with a case of quintessential niceness to make good candidates for Christianity. But the very attitudes that make them "nice" non-Christians may make them "nice" Christians as well—and by "nice" I mean lukewarm, insipid, unoffensive, and harmless. As much flavor as tea brewed from yesterday's leaves. As much color as a smogged-over skyline. As much appeal as cold oatmeal.

Deliver us!

Jesus had the disturbing habit of offering God's help to the flagrantly un-nice. Tax collectors. Political revolutionaries. Prostitutes. Winebibbers and gluttons. And of these people He made saints, rugged soldiers of the Cross who were willing to live and die for Him.

Perhaps we need to take a second look at our prayer lists and be sure they include a Saul or two. Their conversions may be unusual, but they aren't impossible.

His Conversion Happened Suddenly and Dramatically

Paul was blinded by a light from heaven, and his life instantly made a 180-degree turn, from persecutor to preacher, in a flash! For most of us, that isn't how it happens. Most often God works to draw us slowly and quietly into His life.

God took Elijah to a mountainside to see His glory. A windstorm shook the mountain, but God wasn't in the wind. Then an earthquake rumbled, and then a great fire blazed. But God wasn't in any of these dramatic manifestations. No, God showed Himself in a still, small voice. And that's often how it is today.

Most of the people I see come to Christ do it in a process. They study, they inquire, they attend, they read, they listen, they ask, and gradually they come to a point of saying yes. I see them exhibit growing curiosity and honest doubt as they move toward commitment. And very often there is a moral, ethical turning that precedes conversion, which I believe reflects the feeling that "some of the things I am doing are wrong. I'm going to try to stop." Then comes a moment of truth, when the person says, "Yes, Lord, I give You permission to control my life." Coming to Christ involves more searching than it does skyrockets.

But we do need to give God room to send skyrockets if He so chooses. Our God of the still, small voice *does* also speak through burning bushes, as He did to Moses, and appearances of angelic messengers, as He did to Mary. If we're part of a belief system that allows no spaces for anything but plodding and planning, we may have rationalized God out of our faith.

When I was working as a field representative for the Billy Graham Evangelistic Association film ministry, I remember an encounter in which God chose to be dramatic.

Usually, these Gospel films were shown in one city at a time. But we'd decided to take a stab at showing the film at twenty-seven different theaters, all in the same week. The idea was bold, especially since we had a staff of only five to execute it. As you can imagine, the five of us were working twenty-six hours a day coordinating the events. That's why we refused when someone called from Wallace, North Carolina (population 1,000) and asked us to show the film there.

We had every logical reason to decline. Besides our understaffing problem, we were only showing the film in commercial theaters, and the movie house in Wallace had long since closed.

However, the citizens of Wallace persisted. They soon called back to say they'd reserved the high school gym to show the film. Now would we come?

We refused again. Using a school gym would involve setting up a twenty-eight-foot screen and operating two projectors to handle the two-reel film. All this would require the work of an extra man, one we simply couldn't spare. That was that.

But within days, we got a call from our home office. It seemed that folks in someplace called Wallace, North Carolina had made known their intense displeasure that we wouldn't come and show the film for them. Would we see what we could do to honor their request?

Well, logic is one thing, but "strong encouragement" from headquarters is another, so we packed our equipment and headed for Wallace. And to our red-faced delight, nearly the entire city attended, and dozens of people accepted God's invitation to give their lives to Christ.

A twelve-year-old named Linda was one of those to respond. That night after the film she wrote in her diary, "Today is the most wonderful day of my life. I accepted Jesus as my Saviour. I have never been so happy!"

That night would be Linda's last on earth. The very next day, on the way home from school, Linda was abducted and brutally murdered. When her father wrote to tell us the tragic news, he closed his letter by saying, "Thank you for coming in time for Linda."

God pushed and prodded to overrule our logical guidelines because He knew the urgency of the moment for a little girl's eternal destiny. We need to leave room in our lives for divine intervention, sometimes miraculous intervention, as God works out His purposes.

Paul Caught an Unusual Glimpse of the Lord

Paul confirmed to his brothers in Corinth that many had seen Christ after His resurrection. First Peter saw Him, then the Twelve, then 500 brethren, "and last of all, as it were to one untimely born, He appeared to me also" (1 Cor. 15:8). Here Paul makes it plain that on the road to Damascus, he didn't just hear the Lord's voice; he actually saw the Saviour for himself.

Since His ascension to heaven, Christ has rarely appeared on earth to anyone. I believe it happened here because God intended that Paul become the twelfth apostle, replacing Judas, the betrayer. But as Paul said, he was born at the wrong time. In order to qualify as an apostle, it was necessary to have seen the Lord (Acts 1:21-22), but without this miraculous encounter with the risen Christ, Paul could never have fulfilled his calling to apostleship.

Most will never see the Lord as Paul did, yet we see Him in the lives of those in whom He dwells. And those who don't know Him see Christ in those of us who do.

Paul's spiritual birth had unique qualities, but three facets of his conversion are *common* to us all.

Like All Conversions, Paul's Originated with God

When Paul was converted, nobody could take credit but God. No one could say, "We were having a great revival meeting, and I preached a terrific sermon." No one could brag about what a wonderful job the choir did singing the anthem before Paul was converted. No one could boast, "I invited him to a Christian Businessmen's Club luncheon." His change of life was all God's doing, but it was no more of God than the conversion of the smallest child in a Bible school. If any of us claim that salvation is the result of our doing, then we've made salvation less than salvation.

We know Christ because, and only because, of the supernatural invasion of God into our lives. We take far too much credit for coming to Him, because in reality, He does it all.

A.W. Tozer, the great preacher whose writings have guided many in their quest for God, said this:

> Before a man can seek God, God must first have sought the man. We pursue God because, and only

because, He has first put an urge within us that spurs us to the pursuit. "No man can come to Me," said our Lord, "except the Father which hath sent Me draw him," and it is by this very prevenient *drawing* that God takes from us every vestige of credit for the act of coming. The impulse to pursue God originates with God, but the outworking of that impulse is our following hard after Him; and all the time we are pursuing Him we are already in His hand" (A.W. Tozer, *The Pursuit of God,* Christian Publications, Inc., pp. 11–12).

Years ago, my five-year-old son Mark and I spent an afternoon together flying a model airplane. It was one of those days a kid lives for—sun sparkling above, our airplane buzzing overhead, and both dad and son totally enjoying being together. As we brought the plane in, Mark looked up at me and sighed, "Gee, Dad, I sure am glad that I picked you out to be my father!"

He'd learn in the years to come that he didn't pick me out at all, but I knew how he felt because I have felt like that toward my Heavenly Father. Sometimes I have prided myself on being smart enough to choose Him, when in reality He's the One who did the drawing to bring me to Him.

We seek Him, but He moves our heart to do so. How grateful we can be that Christ wooed us and courted us and pursued us until He won our hearts!

Like All Conversions, Paul's Came Totally by Grace

Listen to this: "For by grace you have been saved through faith; and that not of yourselves, it is the gift of God; not as a result of works, that no one should boast" (Eph. 2:8-9).

Salvation always comes from God's grace to us, never as a

reward for our goodness. It is never a response to how hard we try or how much religious fervor we demonstrate. God won't be manipulated by our goodness. How could He, when "all our righteous deeds are like a filthy garment"? (Isa. 64:6) When any of us become converted, it's always because God has chosen to act toward us in grace. He gives us a gift we can't earn or merit. *His* goodness, not ours, is the foundation for true conversion. If we had to depend on ourselves, we'd all wind up lost eternally because everyone has sinned, and the payment we've rightfully earned for our sin is death. Eternal life comes as God's free gift to us, a gift of His grace, even though we sometimes think the credit belongs to us.

My friend Charlie Langelle grew up as part of a street gang in St. Louis, and just as in most gangs of the eighties, the boys in this one knew how to play rough. (One of Charlie's former pals from the gang now serves a life sentence for murder in a Marion, Illinois prison.) But grace invaded Charlie's life. His wife Jean heard the Gospel at a neighborhood Bible study and, as a result, wound up attending our church. Through her initiative, Charlie came too, and both Jean and Charlie met the Lord. Charlie is now a deacon in that church, and his gentle spirit defies any identification with that tough street-kid he used to be.

God's grace motivates Him to initiate our salvation. It isn't the other way around.

Paul's Life Was Transformed

When Paul met the Lord, God removed his anger, hatred, and bitterness. When I meet people filled with hostility, I sometimes wonder about the genuineness of their faith because hostility and godliness can't live together. Scripture reminds us that "even so, faith, if it has no works, is dead" (James 2:17). A change in belief brings a change in life.

Saul was so filled with hatred that he had no qualms about putting Christians to death. But this same bitter man was transformed into the author of 1 Corinthians 13, the love chapter. And he told the church members in Thessalonica, "We proved to be gentle among you, as a nursing mother tenderly cares for her own children. Having thus a fond affection for you, we were well-pleased to impart to you not only the gospel of God but also our own lives, because you had become very dear to us" (1 Thes. 2:7-8). From murderous hatred to the tender affection of a nursing mother! That's a transformation!

I know a man in southern Missouri who owned two liquor stores. After he was converted in a revival, he went home and put those stores up for sale. One of the stores sold, but the other one didn't, even after multiple attempts to get rid of it. Finally, the man decided he could keep the store but simply get rid of the booze, so he moved out the liquor and restocked it as a hardware store.

Later, a scoffer was taunting him about his faith. "Do you really believe Jesus could turn water into wine?"

The man replied quietly, "I don't know about that, but I can tell you one thing: I know He can change a liquor store into a hardware business!"

Conversion transforms us. God initiated the work by providing for Christ's death to pay the penalty for our sin. All we need to do is respond to His initiative with faith.

CHAPTER EIGHT
Cornelius—The God-Fearer

The doctor glowered at Ed Banks over the top of his bifocals. "You say you're not taking the medicine I prescribed to control your high blood pressure?"

His patient shrugged his shoulders. "Look, Doc," he countered. "Medicine is for sick people. I was careful to take it while that problem with high blood pressure flattened me. But now I feel great. Why should a man who can work all day and still play six sets of tennis at night need to take medicine?"

Doctor Williams cleared his throat. "Ed, your good behavior is keeping those symptoms well controlled, but you're a sick man, whether you look like it or not. Without the proper treatment, that high blood pressure will kill you, just as surely as it'll kill someone who's on his back in the hospital. Just because you're not showing symptoms doesn't mean you don't have a disease."

Are you shaking your head at Ed Banks' ignorance? Don't condemn him too quickly; you may be guilty of making the same mistake when it comes to the disease of sin. The Bible says that sin is a problem we all have to face. But we're not so sure. We look at murderers, adulterers, and pornographers and agree these are sinners. But when we see a moral man, we hesitate. Is he a sinner in need of conversion? We may hedge on our answer, especially when his good behavior already outshines the good deeds of many Christians we know.

But like the doctor we just met, Christ is a concerned Physician who doesn't bluff His patients. He makes it clear that we're all dying of the disease of sin, even though we may not show many symptoms of being sinners.

Cornelius was just such a well-behaved sinner. He feared God and led his household to do the same, gave generously of his goods, and even practiced times of personal prayer. Few symptoms of sin there. But God knew good works wouldn't save him; only Christ could do that.

> Now there was a certain man at Caesarea named Cornelius, a centurion of what was called the Italian cohort, a devout man, and one who feared God with all his household, and gave many alms to the Jewish people, and prayed to God continually. About the ninth hour of the day he clearly saw in a vision an angel of God who had just come in to him, and said to him, "Cornelius!" And fixing his gaze upon him and being much alarmed, he said, "What is it, Lord?" And he said to him, "Your prayers and alms have ascended as a memorial before God. And now dispatch some men to Joppa, and send for a man named Simon, who is also called Peter; he is staying with a certain tanner named Simon, whose house is by the sea. . . ."
>
> And opening his mouth, Peter said: "I most certainly understand now that God is not one to show partiality, but in every nation the man who fears Him and does what is right, is welcome to Him. . . ." While Peter was still speaking these words, the Holy Spirit fell upon all those who were listening to the message. And

all the circumcised believers who had come with Peter were amazed, because the gift of the Holy Spirit had been poured out upon the Gentiles also (Acts 10:1-6, 34, 44-45).

Setting the Stage

Every person's birth is miraculous, but some lives are more pivotal than others in shaping the direction of history. So it was with the spiritual birth of Cornelius. Any person who comes to Christ sets off peals of rejoicing in heaven, but Cornelius' conversion was one of a kind because it marked the opening of the door of salvation to the Gentiles. Until then, the apostles understood that new life came by Christ, but they thought the path to Christ had to wind through Judaism. Adhering to the Jewish religion was a necessary stepping-stone to embracing Christianity.

Then came the day the Apostle Peter was waiting for lunch on a rooftop in Joppa. There he saw the famous vision of a sheet let down from heaven, full of animals considered unclean by Jewish tradition. Three times he was told to eat the animals; three times he refused, pleading obedience to the Jewish Law. Three times a voice rebuked him: "What God has cleansed, no longer consider unholy."

As he awoke and puzzled the meaning of the vision, a delegation from Caesarea arrived seeking him. They took Peter to meet the Gentile, Cornelius. When Peter told him about Christ, he responded gladly and God received him. Then Peter understood the message of the vision: God was inviting *all* who had faith to come to Him, not merely the Jews.

From this episode, the other apostles also became convinced that God was extending salvation to the Gentiles by faith alone.

His conversion made Cornelius as unique as the first man to

join the National Organization of Women or the first white to be part of the NAACP or the first ACLU attorney to pledge his support to the Moral Majority. This Roman commander paved the way for Gentiles like you and me to come to Christ without having to first become Jews.

Even Moral People Need Conversion

Cornelius was a good man in a job where being good didn't come easily. As a Roman centurion, he led a troop of 100 men. On the whole, centurions were rough and hard-edged soldiers, like the steely-eyed master sargents of today's army or the navy's grizzly chief petty officers. They were unpolished and unbending, better at knocking heads than delicately negotiating. It was likely that a centurion who lived morally had to endure ridicule, just as he might today.

But Cornelius chose upright living anyway. He prayed, he gave generously to those in need, and he pointed those around him to godly living.

A man I know in the Midwest could be a modern-day Cornelius. When Mike was in high school, he was unanimously voted "Mr. Nice Guy" of the senior class, and he deserved it. As valedictorian of his class, ringleader of most school projects, and mainstay of his father's farming operation, Mike won the respect of his classmates and their parents alike.

The next year at college, he met a classmate who shared his passion for basketball, and they began attending all the college games together. But one day his new friend informed Mike he couldn't attend that night's game because he was joining some other students to talk about his faith in Christ.

"Are you a Christian?" the young man queried Mike.

"I like to think I am," Mike replied. He believed God used a balance system when He decided who got into heaven. Mike explained, "I think if your good deeds outweigh your bad ones,

God will accept you. So I'm just trying to keep more piled up on the good side."

They talked more, and Mike found himself intrigued with the idea of talking to others about God. Surely an activity like that would count heavily toward racking up points with God! Maybe it was something he should learn to do, he decided. So he asked his friend if he could join the discussion that night.

His friend agreed, and that evening Mike wound up in the dorm room of another classmate where a Christian student began to share the story of his conversion. As he talked, the collegian they were visiting indicated he wanted to receive Christ as well, so the Christian led him in praying to invite the Saviour into his life. As they prayed, Mike prayed as well. When he heard the Gospel that night, he realized that he'd acted like a Christian in the past, but he had never actually given himself to Christ.

Sometimes I think the hardest people to reach for Christ are good people. Give me a scoundrel any day! Point me in the direction of a rebel who shakes his fist at heaven, and I feel certain he'll soon understand his need of redemption.

But, ah, the upright. How often they use their goodness as a substitute for true conversion, and we let them get away with it. They look converted, and they sound converted, so we pat them on the head and turn our attention to getting the Gospel to those we define as needy.

But God sees the situation quite differently. He doesn't grade on the curve when it comes to testing our degree of sinfulness. His test is strictly pass/fail, and the standard He uses to determine who's acceptable is nothing less than the righteousness of Christ. If He had decided to use a neighborhood poll or a survey of the people at work to determine sinfulness, perhaps the moral individual could meet God's standards; Cornelius certainly would have. But God uses no such measure. He holds us up next to the holiness of God; against this standard not one human being can measure up. Compared to the white-hot purity of His transcendent perfection, our very best efforts at holiness look like buckets of sewage.

Good works may make us more praiseworthy on earth, but they won't get us into heaven. That's why the Lord told Cornelius to find Peter. God knew this devout man *still* needed to find salvation because his good works could point him toward God, but they couldn't convert him. If we could be good enough to earn God's favor, Jesus would never have had to die on the cross. If we could merit salvation by good living, redemption would be in human hands, not supplied by divine intervention.

Devoutness can pave the way for conversion, but when we stand before God, we need something that our devoutness can't give us.

We Must Believe in Jesus to be Converted

Peter told Cornelius, "Everyone who believes in Him receives forgiveness of sins" (Acts 10:43).

In his post, Cornelius was ordered to protect the Roman governor of the province. And the governor of Caesarea turned out to be none other than Pontias Pilate, the man who refused to save Jesus from crucifixion.

When Cornelius sent for Peter, he knew only that Peter would "speak words to you by which you will be saved" (Acts 11:14). God didn't tell him Peter's message concerned Jesus of Nazareth.

How do you think Cornelius felt when he realized that his salvation depended on committing himself to follow the man whom Pilate, his superior, had condemned to death? Perhaps Cornelius wondered if Pilate would order his death as well when he learned that his centurion now claimed Jesus as his God.

Cornelius paid a price when he believed in Jesus, and in doing so, he showed us what true, saving faith is.

We live in an age that claims to be full of belief. We believe in music, in love, in our favorite diet soft drink, in ourselves, in our dog food, and almost anything else this week's batch of television ads tells us to.

But when the Bible talks about believing in Jesus, it means something totally different. Believing in Him means receiving Him, allowing Him to be a living part of me, and giving myself to Him without reservation. It's not just inviting Him to ride in the backseat of my life, allowing Him to offer suggestions now and then as I choose my way. Rather, it's turning the steering wheel over to Him and letting Him set the destination, route, and timing of "my" journey. In fact, genuine belief means striking the notion of "my" journey completely and choosing instead to travel His way.

This kind of costly belief produced the faith that "turned the world upside down." It sparks a faith by which men and women conquer and for which they gladly died.

Cornelius received Christ as his master and encouraged his household to do the same. Genuine belief in Christ leads to commitment.

But it's a commitment God helps us make. One thing Cornelius' story clearly teaches: God will go to incredible lengths to help those who seek Him find His truth. In this instance He sent a vision from heaven not once but three times to Peter, so the apostle would be prepared to take the Gospel to these Gentiles. Then God saw to it that Cornelius knew to send for Peter and that the messengers connected with him. I'll bet the heavenly hosts were kept busy for a good three days in advance trying to get the logistics of this encounter in place! But I'm also sure that seeing all God had done to bring him to faith helped Cornelius say yes to the costly commitment before him.

Conversion Is Sealed by the Holy Spirit

The Bible uses several terms to describe conversion. In Cornelius's case, it is called being given the gift of the Holy Spirit. The Bible also talks about being baptized by the Holy Spirit into the body of Christ or indwelled by the Spirit or sealed by the Spirit or the Spirit bearing witness with our spirit that we are God's children (Rom. 8:16).

All these terms are different ways of expressing the same truth: conversion is a spiritual phenomenon. It is a supernatural event—something which cannot be manipulated by man nor institutionalized by the church.

When a person believes and receives Christ, the Holy Spirit performs a miracle in his or her life. For Cornelius, this new life was first demonstrated by his speaking in an unknown tongue.

Does that frighten you? We live in an age of great confusion about speaking in tongues, but it doesn't have to be so confusing.

Christ's followers first spoke in languages they hadn't learned on the day of Pentecost. Peter explained that this miracle happened to demonstrate the fulfillment of Joel's prophecy: "I will pour forth of my Spirit upon all mankind. . . . and I will grant wonders in the sky above, and signs on the earth beneath. . . . that everyone who calls on the name of the Lord shall be saved" (Acts 2:17-21). And as the Gospel was proclaimed in the native languages of those listening, thousands came to faith in Christ.

It happened again in Acts 8 to a group of Samaritan converts. These new believers were half Jew and half Gentile, so their conversions might have been suspect by the rest of the church. When they received the gift of tongues first unveiled at Pentecost, Jesus' followers knew God had received these Samaritans. And for the Samaritans, they now had a tangible source of clear identity with the apostles and the Jerusalem church, so there could be no division between them.

It also happened with Cornelius, the first Gentile convert.

I believe this demonstration of speaking in tongues was God's way of authenticating the fact that the Gospel was for all people, Jew and Gentile alike. The period of the early church, and these instances we've discussed, represent unique junctions in Christian history in which God worked in unique ways to make His direction unmistakably clear. But that doesn't mean this experience of tongues will come on you today.

The moment you receive Christ, you also receive His Spirit. The Holy Spirit uses two vehicles to demonstrate His presence in our lives. He gives us His *gifts* to use in service (as 1 Corinthians 12 explains), and He brings forth His *fruit* of love and joy and peace and all the rest in our lives (Gal. 5:22-23).

The Spirit gifts each of us uniquely. He will direct some to preach, others to give, others to show mercy, others to exercise great faith, others to serve in different kinds of ministries. But, "to each one is given the manifestation of the Spirit for the common good" (1 Cor. 12:7).

Like symphony orchestra musicians, we're all given different instruments to play so that in the blending of our melodies, the music of God may be heard in all its richness around the world. An orchestra *must* have different instruments to make a full-orbed sound, but each of those instruments must be following only one conductor. So it is with Christ's followers: "Now there are varieties of gifts, but the same Spirit. And there are varieties of ministries, and the same Lord. And there are varieties of effects, but the same God who works all things in all persons" (1 Cor. 12:4-6).

But the Spirit's gifts aren't the only way He makes known His presence in a believer's life. More important, He confirms that we belong to God as He brings forth His *fruit* of love, joy, peace, patience, kindness, goodness, faithfulness, gentleness, and self-control in our lives. If we're rooted in Him, this fruit will appear on our branches. I sometimes hear new converts report, "I'm feeling love for people I never could before," or "My children don't rile me up like they used to," or "I'm making progress against a bad habit that's plagued me for years." When they say such things, I shout a silent "hurrah!" because I know I'm seeing the Spirit making His presence and power known in their lives.

The Spirit's gifts and His fruit make it clear to us and others that God Himself has come to live in us, just as the gift of tongues assured Cornelius *and* the apostles that this devout Gentile now unquestionably belonged to God.

I recently read someone's observation that we're investing too much energy fighting about whether or not the church should speak in an unknown tongue. The truth, this writer said, is that the church *is* already speaking in an unknown tongue. With all our holy buzzwords, in-house language, and sectarian squabbling, those outside the faith haven't the slightest idea what we're about and wouldn't recognize the Gospel if it moved in next door to them! I deeply fear this writer has an excellent point. We quibble back and forth over minor issues while the world in which we live careens headfirst into a godless chasm.

Let's get on with proclaiming and explaining and wooing people to the Gospel. Christ isn't willing that anyone perish, and we shouldn't be either. Some we reach will be reprobate; others will smell as clean as Cornelius did. Both need conversion, and conversion can transform both into new creatures in Christ.

CHAPTER NINE
Thief on the Cross—The Undeserving One

I wonder how many world records in sports have been missed by a runner or a skier or a skater coming in just a hundredth of a second too late. And how many millions of dollars have been lost on Wall Street because a stock broker put off calling in a "sell" or "buy" order until the next day. And how often stroke victims have died because help arrived minutes too late.

Procrastination may have devastating consequences in many arenas of life, but as long as we have breath, it's never too late to be converted. God continues to extend His grace even to the last moments of our lives. Because He does, a dying thief found eternal life.

One of the criminals who were hanged there was hurling abuse at Him, saying, "Are You not the Christ? Save Yourself and us!"

But the other answered, and rebuking him said, "Do you not even fear God, since you are under the same sentence of condemnation? And we indeed justly, for we are receiving what we deserve for our deeds; but this man has done nothing wrong." And he was saying,

"Jesus, remember me when You come in Your kingdom!" And He said to him, "Truly I say to you, today you shall be with Me in Paradise" (Luke 23:39-43).

Setting the Stage

In his book, *The Last Thing We Talk About,* Joseph Bayly looked back at the deaths of three of his children and reflected:

Birth and death enclose man in a sort of parenthesis of the present. And the brackets at the beginning and end of life are still impenetrable.

This frustrates us, especially in a time of scientific breakthrough and exploding knowledge, that we should be able to break out of earth's environment and yet be stopped cold by death's unyielding mystery. Electroencephalogram may replace mirror held before the mouth, autopsies may become more sophisticated, cosmetic embalming may take the place of pennies on the eyelids and canvas shrouds, but death continues to confront us with its blank wall. Everything changes; death is changeless.

We may postpone it, we may tame its violence, but death is still there waiting for us" (Joseph Bayly, *The Last Thing We Talk About,* David C. Cook Publishing Co., p. 11).

A confrontation with death has an irresistible way of forcing us to look differently at life. Jesus used this truth to help one of his listeners think differently about material possessions.

He told a story of a rich man whose crops produced a harvest so abundant his grain bins couldn't hold it all. Instead of sharing his good fortune, the man decided this crop could buy him peace and freedom. He'd hoard it all and never need anyone or anything again. He decided to tear down his bins and build bigger ones, so he could spend the rest of his days eating and drinking and enjoying life.

But when God wanted to break the man loose from his self-centeredness, He used the most effective tool one could choose—death. "You fool!" God said to him. "This very night your soul is required of you; and now who will own what you have prepared?" (Luke 12:20)

What if you knew your life would end tomorrow? What would you do with the rest of today? Who would you see? What would you say to them? What activities would suddenly become too urgent to postpone another moment?

This was the question the thief had to answer. We're not told his age. Perhaps he was young enough never to have thought much about death. He may have pushed off questions about his eternal destiny for a later time. Now, suddenly, these questions came crashing in on him, and he had to deal with them.

There is an urgency and an electricity about this encounter with Christ because for this man there would never be another chance. And in his experience, we see three factors that prodded him to consider giving his life to Christ, then three qualities of his conversion.

The Thief Prepares for Conversion

1. A change in perspective can prepare us for conversion. In his account of Christ's crucifixion, Matthew gives us an insight to this thief we'd miss if we only read Luke's Gospel. As Jesus hung on the cross, the watching crowd shouted barbarous insults at Him. "He saved others; He cannot save Himself," they sneered. "He is the King of Israel; let Him now come down from the cross, and we shall believe in Him" (Matt. 27:42). They even threw the promises of Scripture in His face, sarcastically quoting Psalm 22:8. "He trusts in God; let Him deliver Him now, if He takes pleasure in Him; for He said, 'I am the Son of God.' "

Then Matthew recounts the final humiliation: "And the robbers also who had been crucified with Him were casting the same insult at Him" (Matt. 27:44). Apparently this dying thief at first joined with others to taunt Jesus. But as the thief hung there, something began to change his opinion. Perhaps it was hearing Jesus ask the Father to forgive His tormenters. The thief knew the bitterness in his own heart and the anger he felt in response to this unbearable pain and humiliation. Yet this man beside him, suffering the same agony, offered forgiveness to those subjecting Him to this agonizing death. For whatever reason, when we read their story in Luke's Gospel, Scripture says only that "*one* of the criminals who were hanged there was hurling abuse at Him" (Luke 23:39). And instead of reviling Jesus, the dying thief now defended Him. He said to the other thief, "How can you curse this man Jesus? Don't you see that He's done nothing wrong?" His hatred had changed to admiration, preparing the way for conversion.

A change of perspective can prepare us for conversion, just as it did for the thief. That's how it happened for Charlie, the sales manager at a Buick dealership in Colorado Springs.

Charlie's wife pulled ligaments in her leg and landed in the hospital for several weeks. Charlie was left to care for the kids and the house and keep up with his own job.

At 6 P.M. the first night Charlie started rummaging in the kitchen, trying to scare dinner out of the cupboards. Just then, the doorbell rang. At the door stood a lady he had never met, delivering supper for them.

"I thought she must be an angel," Charlie said later, "but I didn't see any wings, so I had to abandon that conclusion."

The next night, another woman brought supper. And the next night. And the next.

So he asked his wife, "Who are these people who keep feeding us?" She told him they were women she'd been studying the Bible with, who simply wanted to help.

Charlie said to himself, "If these people are Christians, then they're different from most people I know." So he went to his drawer and dug out a Gospel tract his wife had given him. And he knelt by his bed to tell God, "If that's what Christians are, I want to be like that."

The women's kindness changed Charlie's perspective and opened the door to his conversion (as told by Russ Johnston in *Turn Your Dreams Into Reality,* Victor Books, pp. 79–80).

2. Emotion can precipitate conversion. We live in a generation highly suspicious of mixing emotion and religion. We disdain the hellfire and brimstone preachers of fifty years ago. "Too sensational," we cluck. "They used emotion to manipulate people into the kingdom." And in some cases, we're right in our assessment.

To fortify our stance, we look at Scripture passages like 1 John 4:18: "There is no fear in love; but perfect love casts out fear, because fear involves punishment, and the one who fears is not perfected in love." God doesn't intend us to cower before Him like a jungle native quakes in terror before the erratic destruction spewed out by a volcano.

During the Nazi rule in Germany, the Gestapo conducted a reign of terror. One of their most effective techniques to keep the citizens submissive was undeserved and unprovoked punishment. They'd invade homes at random, dragging off their occupants with no apparent motivation but to prove they had absolute power.

Fortunately, our God isn't like this. In His kingdom, we're not terror-stricken slaves, living in dread of the Master's reprimand, but rather beloved sons and daughters, basking each day in the warmth of His acceptance.

But fear isn't always a bad thing. We use the fear of being kidnapped to keep our children from getting into cars with strangers. We work to make them fear the dangers of alcohol and drug abuse enough to keep away from these killers. Sometimes it's smart to be afraid.

So it is with the fear of God. "Don't you fear God?" the dying thief asked the other criminal, and he asked the right question. God never apologizes for encouraging us to fear Him. In fact, David describes the *un*godly this way: "There is no fear of God before his eyes" (Ps. 36:1).

What is this fear that leads to conversion? I believe it's the overwhelming awe and respect we feel as we see God for who He is. When the prophet Isaiah beheld the Lord, he described Him as "sitting on a throne, lofty and exalted, with the train of His robe filling the temple" (Isa. 6:1). Seraphim surrounded Him, and as they sang of His holiness, the place shook and filled with smoke. When Isaiah experienced God's grandeur, he cried out, "Woe is me, for I am ruined! Because I am a man of unclean lips" (v. 5). That's the fear of God that leads to repentance.

How easy it is for us to trivialize God. I cringe every time I hear someone describe prayer as "talking to the man upstairs." The closer we get to God, the more aware we become of the distance between us. Seeing His holiness makes us fall on our knees and cry, "Oh, God, how can You even consider me? I'm nothing compared to You!" The dying thief began to feel this kind of awe as He beheld Christ's holiness, and he rightly felt a fear of God that prepared the way for his own repentance.

Have you ever experienced this fear of God? Has the light of His holiness ever shown you your own uncleanness? If you have, rejoice, for you may be well on your way to conversion.

3. A guilty conscience can provoke conversion. As the thief glimpsed Christ's holiness, he felt remorse for his own wrong-doing. He told the other criminal, "We are receiving what we deserve for our deeds." Maybe he had never admitted his guilt before this. Perhaps, like most criminals, he kept insisting on his innocence, even after being sentenced to death. But at that moment on the cross he admitted that he had sinned. He didn't just *feel* guilty; he *was* guilty and deserved the punishment he was receiving.

This innate sense of guilt when we do wrong is God's doing. It is His way of motivating us to turn from evil and seek Him. But our age has mixed things up. We've decided it's not our behavior that's wrong; it's the guilt we need to eliminate. Pastor/counselor Earl Jabay tells of an encounter with a young lesbian who came to him for help.

"Long ago I liberated myself from all conventional morality. Besides, everyone is bisexual, so what difference does it make whether I go to bed with a man or a woman?"

"I'm puzzled," I responded, ignoring her question, "as to why you asked to see me."

"Well, it's that I *do* feel guilty about being a lesbian, even though I should not. There's no reason to feel ashamed, and yet I am. Why do I feel this way?"

I tried to explain, without much success, that she knew very well that she was breaking God's laws with her sexual conduct. "I know you feel guilty. You are *supposed* to feel guilty when you break the commandments of God" (Earl Jabay, *The Kingdom of Self*, Bridge Publishing, Inc., p. 49).

Guilt feelings may actually be one of our great allies if we allow them to lead us to Christ. That is, after all, what they were created to do. Jesus didn't come to make us wallow in guilt. He said of Himself, "For God did not send the Son into the world to judge the world, but that the world should be saved through Him" (John 3:17). His purpose is not to make us feel guilty but to cleanse our sins, so we've no reason to feel guilty anymore. But the cleansing can only begin when we own up to our sins, what the Apostle John calls "confessing our sins."

He puts it this way: "If we confess our sins, He is faithful and righteous to forgive us our sins and to cleanse us from all unrighteousness." But, "If we say that we have not sinned, we make Him a liar, and His word is not in us." And, "If we say that we have no sin, we are deceiving ourselves, and the truth is not in us" (1 John 1:9, 10, 8).

Bible commentator Charles Ryrie says this about confession. "*Confess* means to say the same thing about sin that God does" (*Ryrie Study Bible*, p. 1879). We often say a number of things about our sins that don't match God's assessment, however.

We may recategorize our sins as "problems" or "struggles." ("I have a real problem with anger or jealousy or self-pity.") This can be a clever move, since Scripture never requires that we confess problems, only sins.

Or we may spend all our time confessing *others'* sins. ("Please pray for me. My daughter's husband is running around with another woman, and it's causing me such despair I can't function.") My life may be full of problems, but they're always other people's problems.

Or we agree we've sinned, but shift the responsiblity for our sin to someone else. ("My father abused me as a child, and that's why I can't seem to say no to immoral relationships.") If this reasoning were true, then 100 percent of abused children would inevitably become immoral adults, and many don't. We can also make choices about our own behavior, though wounds from the past may make some paths more difficult to select than others.

The thief on the cross agreed with God about his past. His deeds violated God's laws; they were sin, and he was wrong to have done them. The guilt he felt was warranted, for he was, indeed, guilty. Having confessed, he became a ready candidate for conversion.

The Thief Begins the Process of Conversion

1. Conversion begins with an expression of faith. "Lord, remember me when You come into Your kingdom."

Three men hung on crosses, dying criminals' deaths. Yet the thief looked at Jesus with eyes of faith and saw Him as something different. To human eyes He appeared to be just as the other two—weak and helpless. But the thief showed incredible faith in Christ with two statements. First, he called Christ Lord. Amazing! To everyone, Jesus appeared just as vulnerable and powerless as the two thieves. But the thief said, "No. You are different from us. You are the Lord, Someone above us, Someone worthy of our allegiance."

He also affirmed his belief in Christ's kingdom. Many believed in Christ's kingship when they witnessed a dramatic healing or saw the dead spring to life at His command. This was certainly a heavenly king in action. And it was easy to affirm His rightful kingship as multitudes waved palm branches and shouted hosannas during His triumphal entry into the Holy City.

But this thief looked at the broken, bleeding form of Jesus dying on the cross and, with eyes of faith, saw the King of heaven. And he called on the King to remember him.

Perhaps you're wondering if the thief's plea is the one you should use to enter Christ's kingdom.

The Ethiopian eunuch gave what most would consider a very classic expression of faith when he affirmed, "I believe that Jesus Christ is the Son of God" (Acts 8:37). But Scripture gives us all kinds of examples of affirmations of faith to which Christ responded. One father said, "I do believe; help my unbelief!" (Mark 9:24) Peter and John didn't say anything at all when they left their nets and followed Christ. Apparently their act of obedience was expression enough of faith.

A genuine expression of faith can't be reduced to a proper liturgical form. If it is, we rob faith of its vitality. We can print the "right" call to conversion in the order of a worship service and have you read it with eloquence and accuracy, but that won't result in conversion. The new birth begins with a cry from your innermost being: "Lord, I'm guilty. Remember me! Save me!" The call of faith, not the vocabulary, is what opens heaven's doors and makes salvation a reality.

Happily, it isn't necessary to say, "Remember me" to be converted. Your declaration of faith in Christ can come in your own words, just as it did for the thief. You may find yourself saying something as simple as, "Jesus, whatever it is that you do, I give you permission to do it."

2. Conversion comes in an instant. When the thief called to Jesus, the Lord promised him, "Today you shall be with Me in Paradise." He didn't say "tomorrow." He didn't say, "You will have to wait a few weeks." He didn't say, "You will have to spend a few years somewhere else paying a price."

A conviction of our need for new life may take days or weeks or years to build, but when conversion comes, it happens instantly. It's much like human birth. Conception occurs, and nine long months go by. (I'm told no one knows the meaning of time standing still better than a woman eight and a half months pregnant!) But then comes the moment of birth. Salvation can come in the same way. The Spirit·implants God's truth, and a period of gestation follows as we come to understand our need of Christ. But suddenly that moment comes, and faith says, "Yes, I believe!" That is conversion.

3. Conversion comes with assurance. God wants you to know if you're converted or not. Jesus assured the thief, "Today you *will* be with Me in Paradise." He left no questions, no doubts. The issue was settled; their pact was sealed for eternity. Christ knew it, and He wanted the thief to know it too.

Not all of us remember our moment of spiritual birth. I confess I have trouble remembering my moment of physical birth (of course, I have a good excuse, since I was very young at the time). But sometimes not remembering our conversion can cause us to doubt whether or not it has really happened.

I have talked to many people who could not give a time and date for their spiritual birth, but that doesn't mean they haven't been reborn. They may be uncertain of the past, but they can always be certain of the present. I ask, "What is your condition now? What is your present relationship with Christ?" For some, that assuages all doubt. They glow with assurance of their closeness to the Lord and His pleasure in them. They may not remember a spiritual birthday, but they're breathing and growing and thriving spiritually, so any questions about the date of their birth seem irrelevant.

But others aren't as certain. To them, I offer this encouragement. There's no need to live under the confusion of doubt. If there's any question about your conversion, the issue can be settled at once by simply making a present commitment to Christ, asking Him for forgiveness, and giving yourself to Him. Even if the past is difficult to unravel, and the future is uncertain, we can operate in the now. We can settle any questions by committing ourselves to Him now. If we've never been reborn, a present commitment will send us into tomorrow filled with assurance instead of doubts.

CHAPTER TEN
The Prostitute—The Immoral One

In twentieth-century America, our prime goal seems to be becoming need-free. Master Card promises our financial freedom, and becoming our own best friend guarantees our relational freedom. We want to live pain-free with the help of extra-strength headache remedies. Valium and IMT both help insure we'll be worry-free.

Unfortunately, Scripture portrays our God as one who has little time for those who think they have arrived spiritually or financially or emotionally.

But give Him a person in need, and He springs into action. Let a weary, burdened one come to Him, and He delights to give rest. Let the hungry or thirsty or poor or sick approach Him, and He springs to their aid. When the guilty or lonely or afflicted or oppressed seek Him out, He loves to rescue them. Never once do we find Him sending a seeker away because the needs before Him seem too many to meet. When the Pharisees criticized Jesus for associating with taxgatherers and sinners, He said, "It is not those who are healthy who need a physician, but those who are ill" (Matt. 9:12).

He showed He meant what He said one day when instead of courting Israel's elite, He chose to focus His attention and acceptance on an immoral woman who needed Him.

> Now one of the Pharisees was requesting Him to dine with him. And He entered the Pharisee's house, and reclined at table. And behold, there was a woman in the city who was a sinner; and when she learned that He was reclining at table in the Pharisee's house, she brought an alabaster vial of perfume, and standing behind Him at His feet, weeping, she began to wet His feet with her tears, and kept wiping them with the hair of her head, and kissing His feet, and anointing them with the perfume. Now when the Pharisee who had invited Him witnessed this, he said to himself, "If this man were a prophet He would know who and what sort of person this woman is who is touching Him, that she is a sinner. . . ."

> And turning toward the woman, He [Jesus] said to Simon, "Do you see this woman? I entered your house; you gave Me no water for My feet, but she has wet My feet with her tears, and wiped them with her hair. You gave Me no kiss; but she, since the time I came in, has not ceased to kiss My feet. You did not anoint My head with oil, but she anointed My feet with perfume. For this reason I say to you, her sins, which are many, have been forgiven, for she loved much; but he who is forgiven little, loves little." And He said to her, "Your sins have been forgiven. . . . Your faith has saved you; go in peace" (Luke 7:36-39; 44-48; 50).

Setting the Stage

Sometimes it's difficult to learn the ways of God, when His ways stand in diametric opposition to the ways we do things. A prime example is the issue of neediness.

David Mains sees this in the issue of spiritual dependency:

> Unlike earthly parents, our Heavenly Father measures our spiritual maturity by the amount of dependence we choose to place on Him. God is the perfect parent and when we look at His example we can draw lessons, if we are parents ourselves, as to how to raise our own children. In the matter of dependence and independence, however, we cannot do what God does. Wise earthly parents raise their offspring to become independent, whole, self-sufficient adults. Conversely, God raises His children to become increasingly dependent upon Him, and this unique relationship is one of the great struggles of the Christian journey (Karen and David Mains, *Parenting Us, How God Does It,* Harold Shaw Publishers, p. 86).

The Pharisees were as nearly need-free as could be imagined. They set the standard for religious life and had cornered the market on God's approval, or so they thought. They had money, status, and power.

Jesus had been invited to dinner at the home of Simon, the Pharisee. Into this situation came the prostitute. For her to enter the house might not have been improper. The Pharisees taught the laws of Israel and therefore lived highly public lives. It was understood that people might come in from the street, stand around the outer tables, and listen to the great words of wisdom being exchanged at these Pharisees' banquets.

But everything about this prostitute stood in contrast to the Pharisee. Simon was a religious professional; she, a professional sinner. He belonged; she was an outcast. He was the standard for acceptability; she met none of the criteria. Both met the Lord, yet she was converted, and he missed heaven altogether.

If you've ever shied away from God because you've felt too needy, let this sinful woman give you courage. She brought her needs to Christ, and in return, had a life-changing experience in conversion.

She Came As She Was

When Luke records the story of this woman's encounter with Jesus, he makes it clear that she was a sinner. Did he find this out several days later when he interviewed her? I don't think so. Her appearance probably billboarded her immoral way of life. Simon the Pharisee could discern her sinful condition simply by observing her appearance and behavior.

But she didn't change her clothes before she came to Jesus, nor did she pretend to be one of the upright matrons of the day. She came to Jesus just as she was, and because she came in faith, He accepted her.

Perhaps she had heard stories of Jesus—how the Pharisees ridiculed Him as a "friend of winebibbers and gluttons"; how He called a hated tax collector to follow Him; the way He came to the defense of a woman caught in adultery. Surely a Man such as this could accept her as well.

Jesus still accepts sinners into His fold. A woman named Iris is living proof.

Iris was a prostitute. No, worse than a prostitute because she managed a nightclub where she could set up "dates" for the girls who worked for her. Into this moral morass entered a Christian who wanted to win her to Jesus. This man "specialized" in sharing Christ with street people, and he chose Iris as his next candidate for conversion. He began coming into her club and telling her in no uncertain terms that she was going to hell and causing others to go there too. Then he'd go to her apartment and witness to her there, leaving all kinds of Gospel tracts when he left. Iris would try to sweeten her coffee, and she'd find a leaflet telling "How to be Born Again" in the sugar bowl. When she unrolled some toilet paper, a Gospel tract he'd stuck up in the paper would float down to the floor. He tried every way imaginable to get the message to Iris.

Apparently, this man had enlisted the partnership of the Holy Spirit in his endeavor because Iris felt more than irritation at his meddling; she felt conviction. Finally, she went to him and said, "All right, you have bugged me long enough. I'm tired of this. I want to become a Christian."

"Fine," he answered. "To do that, you're going to have to get rid of your nightclub and get out of the business of prostitution."

"I'm not going to do that!" Iris protested. "All I want to do is become a Christian."

"You can't become a Christian until you're ready to get out of this life," he insisted. "What's more, when you pray to receive Christ, you will have to do it on the sidewalk in front of your nightclub!"

(I'm glad Iris didn't ask him where Scripture mandated praying on the sidewalk as a prerequisite for salvation. He may have stretched the requirements a bit, but in Iris' case, he was hitting a nerve that needed to be dealt with.)

Iris was furious and insisted she never wanted to see him again. The man left, but the Holy Spirit didn't, and for the next two or three weeks, her misery increased. Finally, she could resist no longer, and she telephoned the Christian.

"I'm ready to receive Jesus," she told him, "but I absolutely cannot do it on the sidewalk in front of my club."

"Then forget it," he said resolutely. "I don't want to talk to you about it."

He was obviously not going to budge, so Iris knew she had only one choice. "All right," she finally agreed, and went to call a cab so that she could meet him at her club. There on the sidewalk in front of the door she got down on her knees and invited Jesus Christ to cleanse her and take control of her life.

Apparently the man who led her to Christ said she ought to go to church, so the next Sunday she swallowed her pride and went. Unfortunately, he didn't tell her she shouldn't dress like a prostitute when she went to church, so when she walked into that Baptist church in a miniskirt, you could hear the eyeballs click! But by God's grace, both Iris and the congregation survived that first Sunday, and today Iris works for the Home Mission Board of the Southern Baptist Convention. She travels all over the United States, giving testimony to what God's power can do.

Like Iris, the sinful woman who came to Jesus came as she was. She didn't try to reform or clean up her act or pretend to be someone she wasn't. She came knowing her only hope rested in His grace and power and His willingness to help her. Deciding to trust His mercy instead of her own goodness paid rich dividends. The Pharisee trusted his own reputation, and missed conversion.

She Was Sorry for Her Sins

David understood God correctly when he wrote, "A broken and a contrite heart, O God, Thou wilt not despise" (Ps. 51:17). This prostitute won Jesus' attention because she demonstrated a broken heart. Her entire posture shouted of humility and repentance. She knelt at His feet, kissing them, and bathed them with her tears. And she soiled her hair to wipe the dust and oil from His feet. This woman was sorry for her wrongdoing.

How fearful we are of mixing emotion and religion! But that's certainly not true in our other passions of life. Author Penelope Stokes shares her experience with a man who feared getting emotional about God, especially when it came to praising Him.

"But I don't know how to praise," one man admitted during an evening Bible study. "I didn't grow up as a Christian, and praise hasn't been a part of my life all these years. I just don't have any experience." But when the home team scores a touchdown, this same man jumps out of his chair, yelling and cheering at the television set. To anyone who asks, he will give a glowing account of the merits of the woman he married. And even those who don't ask are regaled with the exploits of his newest grandson.

We know how to praise. Daily we praise our diets, our cars, our VCRs, our children, our friends, our churches. We extol the value and virtues of the things we cherish most in life" (Penelope J. Stokes, "Toward a Deeper Life of Praise," *Discipleship Journal,* Vol. 7, Number 2, Issue 38, p. 32).

Like this man, we cheer over our joys and weep over life's sorrows. Does it seem out of place, then, that the Lord's kindness might move us to tears?

Of course it wasn't her tears that won this woman forgiveness. Christ said clearly, "Your *faith* has saved you." Perhaps if He hadn't made such a direct assessment, we'd have wrongly concluded that tears are a necessity for true repentance. The nonweepers among us might decide we're without hope of true conversion. Not so. Conversion can be deeply genuine without grandiose displays of emotion. But it's also appropriate that sorrow for our sins will move us to tears. Repentance can take any number of forms, but whatever form it takes, it's a necessary ingredient to genuine conversion.

She Came Away Forgiven

What was this prostitute's biggest need? If she had lived today, what would we have offered as solutions to her problems?

Some would say money would change her life. If she could be guaranteed enough annual income to allow her financial independence, her struggles would be over.

Others would suggest she needed greater self-esteem. They might recommend assertiveness courses and counseling and charm school to help her feel better about herself.

Some would insist she needed a fulfilling career and begin barraging her with aptitude tests and night school applications.

Some would say she needed a good man who wouldn't take advantage of her and set out to fix her up with their cousin Elroy.

Jesus took none of these approaches. He said to her, "Your sins have been forgiven."

The Lord saw this woman with spiritual eyes. He could see the tangled vines of sin strangling her spirit, keeping her from God's holiness and from becoming all she could be.

The English word *holy* derives from an Anglo-Saxon word *hal,* meaning "well" or "whole," and surely there can be no wholeness while the cancer of our sin eats away at us.

Money can solve many problems, but it can't save us from sin. Self-esteem, interesting work, and loving relationships all might make our lives more comfortable, but they can't meet our most basic need: deliverance from our sin. Jesus knew this, so He gave this needy woman the gift she needed most when He forgave her.

God's forgiveness changes us.

A number of years ago, a psychology professor at an Eastern university set about preparing a paper investigating Jesus' statement, "Your sins have been forgiven." He sensed there must be a potent psychological impact inherent in offering someone forgiveness of their wrongs. In preparation for his presentation, he studied the New Testament for source material on the subject of forgiveness.

Though the professor wasn't a Christian when he began, by

the time he finished his research, he had become a case study in his own report. As he presented his findings, he closed with this admission: "I, too, have heard those humble words, 'Son, thy sins are forgiven thee,' and now I am a follower of Jesus Christ." Grabbing hold of God's forgiveness opens the door to a new life.

Jesus stands ready to forgive us; all we need do is ask. Nowhere is His forgiving heart more tenderly portrayed than the story of the prodigal son.

This son turned away from his father's care and rejected his father's wisdom. He deliberately chose a life as opposite as possible from what his father wanted. And he financed his self-destruction with his father's resources. Then, when he had nothing left to bring, he came home, asking forgiveness.

Did his father lecture him or program him into a two-year penance to prove whether or not he was *really* sorry? No. He saw the sorrow in his son's eyes and welcomed him home with open arms. There was no penance, only a party; no reprisals, only rejoicing.

So it is with the miracle of God's forgiveness. When God forgives, He forgets. He promises, "I will not remember your sins" (Isa. 43:25).

When it comes to our sins, God has spiritual amnesia. It isn't simply that He chooses to overlook them for now but stores them away for future reference; He completely wipes them from His memory, and the list is unrecoverable.

A writer I know says that her early experiences with a computer gave her a graphic picture of how completely God forgets our sins. She'd spent a morning spewing out what she was convinced was brilliant prose onto the blank screen. A chapter that should have taken days was half done already, thanks to the help she'd received from all this electronic erasing and editing. Elated, she went to call a friend and brag about her success. But in her excitement, she'd neglected to save the material on a disk. And to her horror, she returned to find her screen blank, her precious words gone. Her curious toddler had thought the orange "reset" button looked inviting, and with one poke, he obliterated the morning's work. And the destruction was complete. There were no crumpled first drafts to refer to, no carbon copies to rely on. The words were gone forever.

When God forgives our sins, it's as if He pushes the orange "reset" button and totally wipes out any record of our wrong. David says He removes our sin as far as the east is from the west (Ps. 103:12). David didn't say He takes them from us as far as the north is from the south. If he had done that, our sins would still be close at hand. Think about it. North and south are only divided by a tiny line called the equator. Therefore, north and south are only inches away from each other. But where is the line that divides east and west? At what point on the globe do you stop going east and start going west? No such point exists, of course. East is infinitely removed from the west, just as our sins are infinitely removed from us.

When God removes our sins, He doesn't leave us empty; He leaves us clean. That's the kind of experience David asked for when he said, "Wash me thoroughly from my iniquity, and cleanse me from my sin" (Ps. 51:2). God responded to David's request and declared him righteous, even though the sins from which David sought cleansing included adultery and murder.

When God forgives, He doesn't simply forget and cleanse; He goes on to restore us. He holds no holy grudges. After David sought forgiveness for his sin with Bathsheba, he said, "Restore to me the joy of Thy salvation. . . . Then I will teach transgressors Thy ways, and sinners will be converted to Thee" (Ps. 51:12-13). David sinned dreadfully, but when He confessed, God went on to bless his final years and even used his sin to teach generations of believers how to respond when they do wrong.

Of course, David paid a price for his sin. The child he and Bathsheba conceived in sin died, and David struggled with family problems the rest of his life. But he experienced the Lord's comfort in the death of his child, and later God brought from his union with Bathsheba a son named Solomon, who would succeed David to the throne of Israel and be mightily blessed of God.

When we seek God's forgiveness, He responds, not because we deserve it, but because He is faithful and just. He's decided that Christ's death would wipe out the penalty for our sins, so when we call on Christ, God is obligated by His justice to forgive and cleanse us.

The prostitute in a house of the Pharisees experienced just such cleansing and restoration. This moral outcast became an acceptable member of God's household and was given a clean slate on which to write the story of her life.

Do you need cleansing? Are there wrongs in your past that strangle you and keep you from knowing God's peace and joy? Christ stands as ready to forgive you as He was to grant absolution to the prostitute. He only requires you to come to Him with a repentant heart, as she did.

CHAPTER ELEVEN
Philippian Jailer—The Desperate One

Jesus showed special concern for prisoners in jail, but few of us take time to share His burden. Perry and Mary Ann Jordan are an exception. This quiet couple decided they couldn't solve all the prisoners' problems, but they could do a little, so they began visiting jails near them to tell prisoners God loved them. Soon they were looking for new ways to make His love real. That's how the Christmas Cookie Ministry began. If "nothin' says lovin' like something from the oven," the Jordan family must overflow with love, because last year they distributed baskets with some 90,000 cookies in them to prisoners in Florida jails. Their kindness was so well received that the governor of the state has officially welcomed them into any jail in Florida where they'd like to work. But more important, last year through those cookies and the Gospel tracts that accompanied them, some 240 prisoners met the Lord.

One of these criminals who prayed to receive Christ was released shortly after. He found living on the outside tough going. All his attempts to find work failed, and finally, without money and feeling desperate, he decided to rob a 7-Eleven convenience store. He stuck a gun in his boot and entered the store. Once inside, he bent over to reach for the gun, but when he lifted his head, he found himself staring straight into the cookie rack! Memories of the Jordans' cookies and the commitment he had made to Christ flooded over him, and he turned and left the store. Three days later he got a job as a truck driver and began a new life.

The Book of Acts records the story of another conversion just as transforming. But this time the subject isn't a prisoner. It's the prison warden.

The crowd rose up together against [Paul and Silas], and the chief magistrates tore their robes off them, and proceeded to order them to be beaten with rods. And when they had inflicted many blows upon them, they threw them into prison, commanding the jailer to guard them securely; and he, having received such a command, threw them into the inner prison, and fastened their feet in the stocks. But about midnight Paul and Silas were praying and singing hymns of praise to God, and the prisoners were listening to them; and suddenly there came a great earthquake, so that the foundations of the prison house were shaken; and immediately all the doors were opened, and everyone's chains were unfastened. And when the jailer had been roused out of sleep and had seen the prison doors opened, he drew his sword and was about to kill himself, supposing that the prisoners had escaped. But Paul cried out with a loud voice, saying, "Do yourself no harm, for we are all here!" And he called for lights and rushed in and, trembling with fear, he fell down before Paul and Silas, and after he brought them out, he said, "Sirs, what must I do to be saved?" And they said, "Believe in the Lord Jesus, and you shall be saved, you and your household" (Acts 16:22-31).

Setting the Stage

I'm convinced the story of the Apostle Paul would make a great television miniseries. One episode would include more hair-raising experiences and last-second escapes than Indiana Jones could muster in a year. Here in Acts 16, Paul's at it again.

This time, he and Silas land in Philippi, ready to begin the first Christian church in Europe. Their venture begins quietly as they meet Lydia and lead her to faith. But before long they've stirred up the ire of the Philippian authorities. It seems they had cast an evil spirit from a fortune-telling slave girl, and in retaliation, her masters trumped up charges against Paul and Silas and had them beaten and imprisoned.

In the middle of the night, the Lord sends an earthquake to shake open the jail doors and loose their chains. The prison warden, well aware of the punishment ahead for him, decides to save everyone the trouble and commit suicide. But a voice from the dark cell calls out, "Wait! We're all here!" Sure enough, not a prisoner has escaped, and the warden knows he will escape death as well. This incredible escapade leads to his conversion.

Though few of us will experience the drama and trauma the Philippian jailer did, he still has lessons to offer about the new birth. His conversion centers around a big question and a beautiful answer.

The Big Question Is "What must I do to be saved?"

Sometimes in life we miss the answers we need because we aren't asking the right questions. But not this prison warden. After an earthquake rocked his jail, he asked the most important question in life. Three factors brought him to ask the big question about his destiny.

First, he had a *shaking experience*. Literally. The cold breath of the death angel on his neck shocked him into asking about salvation.

Some criticize Christians for "getting religion" in the face of crisis. Of course many of us, like Lydia, don't require a crisis to cause us to think about our relationship to God. But we don't need to apologize if a life catastrophe brings us to Christ. If suffering causes us to consider Christ, then its pain has saved us from the much greater pain of spending an eternity estranged from God, and in that sense, pain can be a good friend.

A couple in Chicago lost their second child through miscarriage. The pain of the loss particularly devastated the young wife, but in the midst of that hurt, she connected with the Lord more deeply than she ever had before. Later she would reflect, "It's been three years since our miscarriage, and I still cry sometimes when I talk about it. But you know, so much spiritual growth came from that painful experience that I almost don't regret having had to suffer." She went on to explain, "Before my miscarriage, I knew about God. I knew what the Scriptures taught about His faithfulness and His help in time of need. But after losing the baby, I experienced the reality of His healing for myself. Watching Him reach into my grief and transform it into peace gave me eyewitness assurance that He is worthy of my trust—and my life" (Maureen Rank, *Free to Grieve*, Bethany House Publishers, p. 169).

Perhaps without the crisis in the jail, this warden might never have considered life and death issues and might never have come to Christ.

A second factor led him to ask about salvation. He *realized he was hopelessly lost*. This warden knew that the same people who showed no mercy to Paul and Silas would show him no mercy either. He was lost with no way out, and death appeared imminent.

When I was sixteen, I learned to fly an airplane, so at age seventeen, I set out on my first solo cross-country flight. In the process of that flight, I became dreadfully lost. There I was, flying somewhere over Illinois in the dead of winter with no idea if I'd ever make it to safety.

Obviously I did survive. I forced a landing in a farmer's field and came away unscathed but shaken to the core. I've not since experienced such massive terror as I did when I realized I was lost and my life might well be over.

It's the kind of terror I see in the eyes of patients as their doctor tells them, "The tumor is malignant," or, "The treatment isn't working."

But we'll never allow Christ to find us until we understand we are lost. The facts are, of course, that all of us stand in the shoes of the Philippian prison warden. We all live with sin's condemnation over our heads, and we're as hopelessly lost as he was if we don't know Christ.

The third factor that led him to ask about salvation was *hearing the Gospel*. If he'd never heard about God's salvation, he'd never have asked for it. When did he hear? Perhaps he listened as Paul and Silas testified in the jail that night. Or he might have heard about Lydia's conversion or the deliverance of the demon-possessed girl.

At any rate, he came to Paul and Silas with the right question. The factors that pushed him to ask that question still operate today. If you know someone in crisis or someone who faces a hopeless verdict or someone who has recently heard the Gospel, you may know a candidate for conversion, just as the prison warden was.

The Answer Is Beautiful

When the jailer asked Paul for help, he didn't receive a theological dissertation. "Believe in the Lord Jesus," was the simple reply, "and you shall be saved." What a classic illustration of getting to the bottom line! Ten words this jailer needed to come to faith—no more and no less.

"Believe," Paul instructed, because salvation comes by faith alone.

"Believe *in* the Lord Jesus," he continued. Don't just believe the truth *about* Him but personally enter into a dependent relationship with Him.

"Believe in *the Lord Jesus*." And He is the Lord, nothing less. Not just a fire insurance policy to protect us from the flames of hell, but the One who must rule our lives right here, right now.

Did you know that another seeker in the New Testament asked the same question the jailer did? In Luke 18, a rich young ruler came to Christ, asking, "What shall I do to inherit eternal life?" In other words, "How can I be saved?" Jesus responded by reminding him of the Ten Commandments.

Of course Christ wasn't saying that keeping the Ten Commandments will guarantee us a spot in heaven. I believe He mentioned these laws of God because He knew the ruler was trusting them for eternal life. Christ started where the young man was. "You know the commandments," Jesus said. To which the young man responded, "All these things I have kept from my youth" (Luke 18:18-21).

Don't you imagine the young man now waited smugly for Christ's praise? To keep all those laws was a laudable feat. Surely this Teacher would slap him on the back and say, "Well done, thou good and faithful servant! Enter into the joy of thy Lord!"

But Jesus made no such response. "One thing you still lack," He said. "Sell all that you possess, and distribute it to the poor, and you shall have treasure in heaven; and come, follow Me" (Luke 18:22).

What? Had the young man heard correctly? Give *all* he had

to the poor? Even the harshest of the Old Testament laws demanded no such sacrifice. Already he gave more to the poor than anyone else in the synagogue. How could this audacious carpenter say he wasn't giving enough!

And leave *everything* to follow Him? Even if this simple Teacher were a messenger from God, following Him would mean forsaking a life of luxury and grace. It was one thing for these poor fishermen and ragtag radicals to leave all for Him; they had nothing to begin with. But he had a beautiful home, a prestigious position, and a life of sophistication. Why couldn't Jesus just encourage him to use his wealth for good purposes and leave it at that like the other rabbis did? Why, meeting the demands Jesus laid down would cost everything he valued most.

"When he had heard these things," Luke said, "he became very sad; for he was extremely rich" (Luke 18:23).

The young man came to Jesus for cheap grace, a spiritual pat on the head, and a word of good cheer. Perhaps he expected Jesus to praise him, as others did, for not letting his immense wealth keep him from dabbling in spiritual concerns. He'd allow Jesus to be his Saviour, his ticket to freedom from eternal damnation, but certainly not his Master. And he turned away from Christ.

What are you grasping so tightly that it means more to you than Christ? How would you respond if He asked you to part with the car you prize or the home you just redecorated or your camper or your savings? What if He asked you to change jobs or move to a new city or leave your profession for full-time Christian work? And what about the people you love? Would you allow Him to take your spouse or your children or your dearest friends? Can He do as He chooses with your health and the well-being of those close to you?

If there is a point in your life at which you'd tell Him no, then He's not your Lord. Choosing Him as master means offering Him a blank contract, with your signature in place at the bottom, and giving Him free reign to fill in the terms. It's committing yourself in advance to a lifetime of saying yes.

Is this a frightening choice? It is—and it isn't. When He is Lord, we give Him freedom to break our hearts, to take from us all that is dearest and closest to us in the world.

But the One we've chosen to follow loves us perfectly, and His love for us pushes away fear. He doesn't demand total authority over us because He's a power-hungry ogre but because He has crafted perfect plans to fulfill our lives, and He needs freedom to accomplish those plans for us, through us, and in us. Whenever the Lord demands something from us, He also reassures us. He told the young ruler, "You shall have treasure in heaven." Christ didn't ask for the man's money so he could be left penniless. Christ intended the man would trade his paltry earthly riches for insurpassable riches in heaven. Jesus wanted to make him richer, not poorer, but lordship was the price.

When first-century Christians were dragged before the Roman court, their salvation lay in pledging their allegiance to Caesar.

"Caesar is lord," the command came forth.

But these followers of Christ would shake their heads. "Jesus is Lord."

Again, the pledge was given. "Caesar is lord," and again, the Christians would respond, "Jesus is Lord."

A third and final time: "Caesar is lord."

"Jesus—Jesus is Lord," they'd say, knowing that with this third refusal, the lions or the torch or the cross awaited them.

Jesus is Lord, and we embrace His lordship when we say "yes" as He calls us to leave our loves and follow Him. "Believe in the *Lord* Jesus," Peter told the jailer.

Then he went on to add the promise. "You *shall* be saved." Not "You might be saved," or "You can hope to be saved," or

"The percentages indicate you have a good chance of being saved." When we promise Christ our allegiance, He pledges His allegiance in return. He will take control of our lives, leading, guiding, empowering, and offering us irrevocable citizenship in His kingdom.

"You shall be *saved*." You won't be just reformed; you'll be redeemed. The old life under Satan's power dies; a new life empowered by God emerges.

The Answer Brought Magnificent Results

The prison warden did believe, and the changes began. At once he began to *reconcile his past mistakes*. Scripture says that very hour he took Paul and Silas and washed their wounds. And just as quickly, he began to *identify with the Lord* by seeking baptism. Also, he became part of a *new fellowship* when he invited the disciples to his home and ate and rejoiced with them. The former enemies were now friends. Those actions are the signs of a healthy spiritual birth!

In Paul, the jailer had more than just an able Gospel presented. He had a good example of Christian living as well. By observing Paul, the jailer could know at once three strategic secrets of the Christian life.

First, following Jesus could land you in jail. This warden came to faith with no illusions. Paul did nothing but follow God's orders and wound up beaten and imprisoned; therefore, I doubt that this jailer came to Christ expecting, as one hymn writer put it, to be "carried to the skies on flowery beds of ease." No one had to explain to him that if we expect to reign with Christ, we must suffer with Him as well. This jailer had seen the raw and bleeding backs of Paul and Silas as he clamped the heavy, metal leg irons around their ankles and left them in the dark, rat-infested cell.

Second, he knew God could miraculously deliver His children. This jailer felt the earthquake and saw the open prison doors. God promises to help His children, and He did it magnificently.

Third, God gave His followers power to sing *while the prison doors were still locked.* Perhaps this is the greatest secret of all. God does deliver us from the woes of life, to be sure. But He also delivers us *in* the woes of life. He gives joy in the midst of sorrow, peace in the presence of pain. We have a hope that lets us sing in the prisons of our lives. Even when our physical deliverance hasn't yet arrived, our spirits can be completely free. Paul and Silas were liberated long before the door to their cell swung open because they trusted in God instead of their circumstances.

And their trust was well founded. Because of, not in spite of, their time in jail, the church in Philippi grew as the jailer and his entire household came to faith. What the enemy intended for evil, God used for great good. He did it for Paul and Silas and their jailer, and He can do it for you as well as you trust in Him.

CHAPTER TWELVE
Andrew—The Witness

Imagine what a frustration it would be to know you've just won the Publisher's Clearinghouse Sweepstakes but then to discover you won't receive the money if you tell anyone else you've won. Groan! When something wonderful comes to us, it's an instinctive response to want to tell others about it.

This is even more true when we come to believe the Gospel. The Holy Spirit who indwells us stirs up in us a desire to glorify God by letting others know what He can do.

So it was with Andrew. He believed in Christ, and the very next day he brought another to the Lord.

Again the next day John was standing with two of his disciples, and he looked upon Jesus as He walked, and said, "Behold, the Lamb of God!" And the two disciples heard him speak, and they followed Jesus. And Jesus turned, and beheld them following, and said to them, "What do you seek?" And they said to Him, "Rabbi (which translated means Teacher), where are You staying?" He said to them, "Come, and you will see." They came therefore and saw where He was staying; and they stayed with Him that day, for it was about the tenth hour. One of the two who heard John speak, and followed Him, was Andrew, Simon Peter's brother. He found first his own brother Simon, and said to him, "We have found the Messiah" (which translated means Christ). He brought him to Jesus (John 1:35-42).

Setting the Stage

John the Baptist preached outside a city known as Bethany or Batha-bara ("Bethany-beyond-Jordan"). It appears that Andrew and his brother Simon had left their fishing business in Bethsaida far to the north and journeyed two days south to hear John's message. Some Bible commentators believe Philip and Nathanael came along as well.

At any rate, Andrew must have been impressed by what he heard about the coming Messiah because he became John's disciple.

John understood his mission to be to prepare the way of the Lord. In his ministry to Andrew, he did just that, for when Jesus passed by, John pointed Andrew to the Lamb of God and Andrew pursued Him. With another man, he asked Jesus, "Rabbi, where are You staying?"

Jesus responded to their interest, not with a sermon but with a supper invitation. Sometime during their evening together, Andrew came to faith. The very next day, he began to tell others of the change in his life.

Andrew Shared the Good News

Remember the lame man sitting by the temple gate to whom Peter and John said, "In the name of Jesus Christ the Nazarene—walk!" (Acts 3:6) When this man was healed, did he slink home in embarrassment? Of course not! Scripture says he began walking and leaping and praising God. Once you've been converted, you naturally want others to know.

The Prophet Jeremiah tried saying no to God's Spirit and decided he'd no longer speak to others about God. But his plan failed miserably. "In my heart [God's truth] becomes like a burning fire shut up in my bones; and I am weary of holding it in, and I cannot endure it" (Jer. 20:9). Trying to quell God's Spirit bubbling up in him took as much energy as trying to put a lid on an erupting volcano, and Jeremiah simply couldn't do it.

It was never God's intent to convert us, then turn us into trophies displayed in a showcase called the church. He saved us to be ambassadors, givers, and proclaimers and then energized us with the Holy Spirit to motivate us for the task. After Andrew believed in Christ, it seemed absolutely natural to take the message to others.

I know how he must have felt. I remember driving my younger brother Joe to the bus station on the day he was to leave for military service. I wasn't sure how this eighteen-year-old would do in the face of temptations inherent in military life. Because our parents had divorced and Joe was eleven years younger than I, I always felt a fatherly sort of care for him. How badly I wanted Joe to be sure of what Christ could do for him! But unlike Andrew, I wasn't sure what to say or how to say it, so I kept quiet as I waved good-bye and watched Joe board the bus.

I got back in my car and started to drive away, but I felt heavy with remorse. Then I could stand it no longer. I wheeled the car around and roared back to the bus, parked, and climbed aboard. Joe looked up in surprise as I came to his seat and slid in beside him. I reached for my New Testament and handed it over. "Joe," I explained, "I love you and I want you to know Jesus loves you too." The urge to remind him of God's care wasn't something someone made me do. God's

Spirit stirred me to want to pass on the wonderful news I'd received.

Andrew Found Peter

Just imagine how quickly Christ could have spread His message if He'd chosen to come to earth during our age of sophisticated communication.

A marketing agency could set Him up with a well-balanced mix of television time, radio spots, newspaper publicity, and mass mailings. Add a satellite link-up and perhaps a snappy video or two, and He could have taken the Gospel to the entire world in a matter of days.

He could have worked this way—but He didn't. He arrived instead at a time when the means of communication was person-to-person. Perhaps His timing tells us something important about the nature of the Gospel. The experience of conversion is a *relational* experience. It isn't simply changing to a new system of thought; it's coming to love and be loved by a Person.

Jesus came to draw us into the embrace of God. This was the purpose of the Incarnation. God wants to be close enough to touch us and be touched by us.

Andrew understood God's passion for relationships. His own conversion came while he was a dinner guest of his new friend, Jesus. And after that encounter, he went out, not so much to evangelize as to make friends and quietly bring those friends to Christ.

After Andrew came to trust Christ, he didn't head for a street corner to preach to a crowd of strangers. He found his brother Simon and brought him to the Lord.

Other Scriptural records of Andrew show this same behavior. He always seems to be connecting with people and helping them make a connection to Christ.

When Jesus saw the hungry crowd of 5,000 before Him (John 6:5-9), He asked Philip how to feed them. Philip threw up his hands in despair at the impossible task. But Andrew stepped into the awkward silence that followed. "There's a little boy here with five loaves and two fish."

Andrew's response shows something about the quality of his faith. Where others saw hopelessness, he could envision possibilities.

But his response says something else as well. I doubt that Andrew heard Christ's question, scanned the crowd for lunch buckets, and pointed out to Jesus a boy carrying one. I'm sure he knew about the boy's lunch because he'd befriended the lad earlier in the day. Once again, he found another and brought that one to Jesus, just as he did with Simon.

Another time, some Greeks came seeking Jesus and, again, Andrew acted as the quiet intermediary.

A ministry like Andrew's is one all of us can have. God intended that the Gospel go to the whole world—one friend at a time.

Andrew Became a Pilot-Light Christian

Some of those Andrew helped went on to do things he simply wasn't called to do. Peter, not Andrew, preached at Pentecost when 3,000 were saved. And it's the little boy who shared his lunch whom we remember when we tell the story of Jesus feeding 5,000. Few even recall that Andrew played a part. Those we befriend who come to Jesus may influence others more than we do. Andrew's witness was like a little pilot light which sets off a flame hundreds of times its own size.

Years ago in Chicago, a Sunday School teacher named Edward Kimball invited a young shoe clerk named Dwight L. Moody to his class. Moody was coarse, rough, uneducated, and a most unlikely candidate for the kingdom, according to

Kimball. But the Sunday School teacher loved him anyway and led Moody to Christ. Moody, of course, went on to become one of America's greatest evangelists. An observer once said, "I think Moody has an option on the Holy Spirit."

"You've got it backwards," the person with him said. "The Holy Spirit has an option on Moody!" And his ministry proved that to be true.

After an evangelistic trip to England, Moody played a part in the life of Winfred Chapman. Chapman became an evangelist and influenced Billy Sunday toward evangelism. Sunday preached to a crowd in Charlotte, North Carolina with powerful results. Later, some of those he influenced invited evangelist Mordecai Ham to hold a crusade in their area.

Before the crusade, the men met regularly to pray that an evangelist of worldwide influence would be raised up from their area. One day, two Charlotte teenagers saw the men heading off into a grove of trees for their prayertime. One asked the other, "What are they doing?"

"Oh, that's my dad and his friends," the other teen said, "praying for an evangelist. And if there's anything the world doesn't need, it's another evangelist!"

That teenager was converted during Ham's revival meetings. His name? Billy Graham (Waylon B. Moore, *Multiplying Disciples,* Missions Unlimited, pp. 16–17).

Few of us will minister like Billy Graham or D.L. Moody, but all of us can play a part in bringing others to Christ.

Perhaps I'm so convinced of this because a quiet witness drew me to the Lord. Though I formally prayed to receive Him in a church service, I was wooed to that service by my wife, who first knew of the Saviour through the friendship of a woman at work.

Early in our marriage, my wife Donna worked in a St. Louis bank, and through a coworker named Dorothy Griffin, Donna heard the Gospel. Donna's exposure to God's truth made her hungry to know more, so she asked me if she could take membership instructions to become part of the church in which I had grown up. I didn't go to the church anymore, but I thought it sounded fine if my wife wanted to, so we called the church and arranged for her enrollment in religion classes.

However, the classes took an unexpected twist. Donna's friend Dorothy made a habit of sharing a Bible study with her during their breaks at work. As Donna's understanding of the Scripture grew, she began to see differences in what the Bible said and what she was hearing at the church's classes. Finally, she came to me to admit reluctantly that she didn't feel she could accept the teachings she was receiving from my church. Would I mind if she began attending the little church to which her friend Dorothy belonged?

I didn't buy into all the religious instruction I'd grown up with either, but I did recall something about tolerance being a virtue, so I agreed to her going to church with her friend.

I can remember today those Sunday mornings when she'd tuck our little daughter into the baby buggy, and I'd hear the clump-clump of that buggy going down the stairs from our second-story apartment as the two of them went to church. I was still in bed, of course, but the clumping of those wheels had a forlorn sound. Until then, Donna and I had shared everything in our marriage, so my wife's spiritual interest became one of our first points of separation, and I wasn't sure how I felt about it.

Donna didn't pester me about coming to church with her, but every so often, she'd drop invitations. "Honey, there are lots of young couples at Dorothy's church. I think you'd enjoy them. Would you like to go with me?" And I'd always agree to go . . . sometime . . . later . . . maybe.

That's why Donna was so surprised one Sunday morning when I got up when she did and dressed for church. We arrived late, and the service had already begun. As we hesitated at the door, the thought occurred to me that these people met in the most pathetic "church" building I'd ever seen. It was made from two old army barracks put end to end and downright ugly. No steeple, no stained glass, no stone.

But oh, the sound of those people singing. I'd never heard anything so alive and vibrant and joyous. It enticed me, but at the same time, I heard a warning bell go off in my head. As we started inside, I whispered to Donna, "By the way, don't get any ideas about me getting saved." I didn't know much about these worshipers, but I'd heard enough jokes and stories about their rambunctious God-involvement to make me a little nervous. But Donna enjoyed them, and I knew she wasn't wacky or pushy, so it would probably be all right.

The preacher, Rev. Earl Pounds, explained the Gospel. And when he finished, he invited all those who hadn't given their lives to Christ to gather at the front of the church so they could pray with him. As he preached, I understood for the first time the purpose of Christ's life and death. And I realized I'd never invited Him into my life. I had experienced religion but had never had a relationship with Christ.

But stand before this gathering of strangers and admit my need? I couldn't do it. I'd just wait until we finished the final hymn and slip out unnoticed.

But the preacher had other plans. He didn't simply remain behind the pulpit and patiently wait for people to respond to Christ's call. He must have taken seriously the Lord's admonition to "go to the highways and byways and compel them to come in," because while we sang, he stepped down and began to walk up and down the aisle, pleading with us to respond. As he passed me, he looked into my eyes and pleaded, "Young man, won't you give your heart to Jesus? Young man, don't go to hell!"

I was feeling more and more inner pressure, and I am sure the hymn we were singing must have had seventeen verses!

But as we finished the last verse, I heaved a sigh of relief. My escape was at hand! But before I could bolt for the door, the preacher took a deep breath and said, "Let's sing it again." Halfway through this second chorus I could resist no longer, and I headed for the front of the church to admit my need for Christ.

The preacher met me and introduced me to a deacon named Fred Ditch, who escorted me to the church basement where he showed me from the Scriptures what it means to receive Christ. Then he looked at me. "Young man, are you serious about giving your heart to the Lord?"

"I've never been more serious about anything in my life," I answered. And kneeling there by a piano bench, I prayed and invited Christ to make me a new person. Some might say that deacon "led me to Christ," but in reality it was my wife who did the leading. If I hadn't trusted her, I never would have ended up in that church where I trusted Christ.

Jesus Converted Peter; Andrew Didn't

When Andrew found Peter, he said simply, "We have found the Messiah." Andrew wasn't responsible to convert Peter, only to expose him to the Lord. All we need to do is let our friends know Christ's love is available and let them see that love in us. God will do the rest.

From the first day Ann visited the diet clinic where she hoped to take off a few pounds, she knew she wanted to share Christ with her counselor. Daily they met for a weigh-in, and daily Ann prayed for a chance to share her faith in Christ, but none ever seemed to open.

"I was starting to feel very guilty," Ann said. "I wanted the woman to know about Christ, but to force the conversation toward spiritual things would have been so abrupt. I didn't know what to do except pray."

But one morning an opportunity came without Ann manipulating anything. As she hopped on the scales to be weighed in, her counselor said, "You know, I am so jealous of you."

Jealous? Ann's mouth dropped open. She'd come in that morning in scruffy jogging clothes and no makeup, with her hair pulled up in a quick ponytail. Surely this beautifully put-together counselor saw nothing in her to be jealous about!

"I'm so jealous," the counselor explained, "of the peace I can see in you."

Ann smiled and gladly told the woman how the Prince of Peace had become the glue that held her life together.

To bring others to Christ we don't need eloquence or great power or much of anything except to quietly let them see Christ. And that may be easier than we think. Our lives radiate much more of Christ's nature than we know they do.

God calls each of us uniquely. Nothing could be clearer from the twelve biblical personalities we've just considered. Each came to Jesus in a slightly different way, but what matters most is that they found the Saviour.

·Some come quietly to Christ, some dramatically. Some come from a moral or religious background, others from a decadent lifestyle. Some are seeking God already when they come; others are running from Him. The rich come and the poor, men as well as women, the expected alongside the unexpected.

But when we come, He receives us and gladly gives us new life as members of the family of God.

If you're not sure of your place in God's family, I pray you will come to Christ, asking Him to forgive your wrongs and give you eternal life. You'll find Him waiting and eager to welcome you.

And if you belong to Him already, I hope you'll open your eyes to those around you. Our world is full of people hungry for an Andrew to befriend them and lead them into a friendship with Christ.